*** FAILSAFE *** LEADERSHIP

55 REASONS WHY OUR LEADERS FAIL

PRACTICAL STEPS TO SUCCESS

MATTHEW ASHIMOLOWO

CONTENTS

INTRODUCTION

The recent failures witnessed in industry by companies like Enron and WorldCom and the catastrophic fall of people like **Bernard Madoff** is a picture of leadership failure.

This trend is repeated in different strata; **Donald Trump**, the paragon of real estate filed for bankruptcy because of business downturn; while spiritual leaders have failed because of character or integrity issues:

Jim Baker – convicted for fraud

Rev. Ted Haggard – admitted to liaisons with another man - even though he had stood against any form of same sex relationship

All these are pictures of leadership failure, and it goes as high as presidencies; President Richard Nixon resigned over the Watergate scandal.

This is leadership failure and it is found in almost every area – business, politics and religion. Many leaders have started from the bottom of the heap but have unfortunately ended up under the heap.

Mighty men have fallen in the past.

The failure of leadership has been registered around the world with the replacement of CEOs because of bad decisions, not listening, failing to make decisions, or making low quality or emotional decisions. Being defensive when a decision has not been beneficial to the organization could also be at the root of why our leaders fail.

> "How the mighty have fallen, and the weapons of war perished!"
>
> **2 Samuel 1:27(The Holy Bible, NKJV)**

Another possibility may be self deception, which makes one think that one is immune and with that attitude ignores all the warnings of the impending possibilities of failure.

In this book I have attempted to deal with the subject and look at many of the reasons why our leaders fail; from the minor to the catastrophic, from the reasons that are seemingly inconsequential, to the ones that cause monumental disasters.

It is not an attempt to celebrate failure but a guide to leaders to pay attention and heed the warning signs.

#1 WHEN THE LEADER HESITATES TO TAKE DEFINITE ACTION

Consensus building is a characteristic of quality leadership. However such seeking of consensus and consulting widely should prepare the leader for making decisions and taking definitive actions. Indecisiveness is the number one kiss of death for leaders. Most great leaders have made their impact in moments of tremendous challenges by taking the bull by the horns at the appropriate time. An unspoken universal law of leadership is that people want their leader to make tough decisions and then lead them forward.

Until June 4, 2010 Yukio Hatoyama was the Prime Minister of Japan. Before his disgraceful exit he came to power from a political dynasty, and promised to make changes which gave the impression that a world changer had arrived. It was not long before it became obvious that he was sky high on promises and paper thin on fulfilment.

When a leader is unable to take action at the appropriate time, he is bidding his career or future goodbye.

When leadership fails to take action and a negative result follows, the buck stops at the table of the leader. It is said that the captain of one of the most historical and sensational shipwrecks – the Titanic - was warned of danger through various radio signals. However he hesitated to make a definitive decision; the result was the ship colliding with a massive iceberg. Most of the leaders who have distinguished themselves before us have been willing to make tough calls.

"All men seek one goal: success or happiness. The only way to achieve true success is to express yourself completely in service to society. First, have a definite, clear, practical ideal-a goal, an objective. Second, have the necessary means to achieve it."

Aristotle

Overcoming inaction, separately as individuals and corporately as a body, may require the creation of timelines for committees and team members. Mechanisms for turning discussions into actions need to be put in place and the leader needs to negotiate the powers to make certain decisions quickly where the situation demands. The leader might also find it necessary to create an Execution Committee.

#2 COMPLAINING ABOUT A LACK OF RESOURCES

While great and qualitative leaders tend to work out how to get the job done with limited resources, leadership failure will often occur because some leaders would rather focus on the resources that are not available and use this as an excuse for inaction.

Resource management is the efficient and effective deployment of an organization's resources when they are needed. Such resources may include financial resources, inventory, human skills, production resources, or information technology (IT). In the realm of project management, processes, techniques and philosophies as to the best approach for allocating resources have been developed. These include discussions on functional vs. cross-functional resource allocation as well as processes espoused by organizations.

Good leadership is known through effective resource management. Leadership is about effective application of the right resources to the right project for profit maximization. It is a mark of matured leadership not to throw money at problems, but to decrease expenses for effective achievement.

Most people have no idea of the giant capacity we can immediately command when we focus all of our resources on mastering a single area of our lives. Anthony Robbins[1].

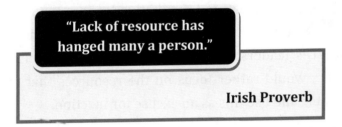

"Lack of resource has hanged many a person."

Irish Proverb

[1] Read more: http://www.brainyquote.com/quotes/keywords/resources.html#ixzz1kzWWHBpV

A leader will either take the responsibility, or declare like **Harry S. Truman** that *"the buck stops here"*.

President Harry Truman had this sign on his desk in the Oval Office. He got the sign from his native Missouri. It was made and sent to him two months after the US dropped the atomic bombs on Japan.

True leadership does not pass on responsibility or blame someone else for the consequences of its decision.

Leadership fails because every single day in business relationships, someone is busy blaming somebody else for the smallest or the most major decision.

All problems have their potential ways out. Admitting the wrong is the first step, and that needs to be immediate.

Identifying the problem and proffering solutions before there are worse consequences is the next step. There should not be a beating about the bush to reduce the enormity of the problem.

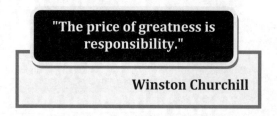

"The price of greatness is responsibility."

Winston Churchill

True leadership means accepting that while you may not deserve the blame, you should shoulder it. You can then take things further in your acceptance of the blame, and work with your leaders in the hope that you will be protected for being truthful and vulnerable.

Once you have caused a problem or are a part of those who caused it, do not wait to be forced to apologise or remedy the situation.

#4

ABUSING THE PRIVILEGES OF LEADERSHIP

An **online encyclopaedia** describes the abuse of privileges as *"when a user performs an action that they should not have according to organizational policy or law".*

During one of my African tours for a series of speaking engagements, the airspace to one particular country had been closed for the presidential jets. The wife of the country's Vice President was arriving in the commercial capital. It was difficult to comprehend how the whole city could be brought to a standstill, and a decision that would hinder the commercial capital of the nation and cause such a colossal loss of money could be made. This is a clear example of abuse of office. It is probably not just the abuse but the numbness of the society to these kind of actions because of their regularity.

When President Nixon authorized the bugging of the room of his opponents, he exceeded his powers and carried out an action he shouldn't have.

The root of the abuse of privileges is when leadership turns around and become dictatorial. In the book *Animal Farm* by George Orwell, Napoleon the pig turned his role from farm leader to dictator. The book captures the gradual transformation of leaders from servants of the people to users of the people. It begins with a delusionary belief by the leader that they are larger than life. From then they are like a monster that cannot be stopped.

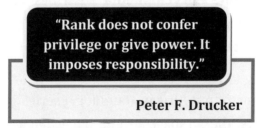

"Rank does not confer privilege or give power. It imposes responsibility."

Peter F. Drucker

It is nobody's fault that these leaders have become corrupt. We cannot hold the electorate responsible for electing the leaders who have turned bad. Corruption and abuse of power is sometimes a by product of greed. Highly placed leaders take their power and use it to abuse people and the position of trust they occupy. At its extreme the abuse of privilege could mean leadership seeing itself as being above the law, carrying out extra judicial actions, acting as if it's one law for the citizens and another for the leaders. There are enough leaders like the late Saddam Hussain, Muammar Gaddafi and so on with enough greed and self absorption to cause adverse results for others, as long as things work for their own myopic interests.

Leadership failure occurs several times because people who end up in power forget they can still come down.

ENGAGING IN THE ACT OF INSUBORDINATION

Genuine and quality leadership will always have a point of reference; somebody who has the powers to checkmate a leader.

Sun Tzu said: *"In warfare, there are flight, insubordination, deterioration, collapse, chaos, and setback. These six situations are not caused by Heaven or Ground, but by the general."*

Most references to this subject is to subordinates who have not been submissive. This is true but the flip side is the fact that it also occurs in leadership circles.

Leadership fails by an act of insubordination or disobedience to such authority or powers constituting to checkmate. Insubordination in this case is purposely ignoring a mentors counsel or instruction. This can often be the result of inexperience or bad judgement, which can itself be remedied with words.

Consider the army general who will not carry out orders, or the young Christian minister who fails to heed the counsel of his overseer but rather launches himself into an independent work; all in the name of the leading of the Holy Spirit.

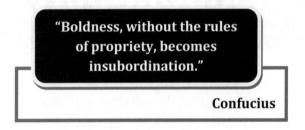

"Boldness, without the rules of propriety, becomes insubordination."

Confucius

In its extreme case, insubordination is manifested through physical confrontation, verbal abuse and a refusal to perform. Leaders who set themselves up for failure regard themselves as being above the expectation of a Board, line manager or mentor.

MAKING SCAPEGOATS OUT OF EMPLOYEES

"A boss creates fear, a leader confidence. A boss fixes blame, a leader corrects mistakes. A boss knows all, a leader asks questions. A boss makes work drudgery, a leader makes it interesting."

Russell H. Ewing

A weak leader plays the blame game and looks for someone else to take the blame; someone else to whom the buck can be passed; someone else who can take the fall when they need to. When that happens leadership has failed.

It is a fact of life that leaders love to hug the limelight when the organization does well. Some leaders go a little further by bragging on how their skills have helped in the progress or success achieved. However, when the ball drops and blame begins to fly, a bragging leader is unlikely to take the blame and will come out looking faultless to their superiors. Just because a leader says a problem is not his fault does not make it true. In reality such stance shows a lack of leadership and ownership on the person's part and in that kind of circumstance, the leader has failed. This kind of leader also likes to lay the blame for any wrong on other people. A bragging leader, who is part of a team, tries to come out looking and smelling like roses if the group gets a matter wrong.

Good leadership would mean to share more credit and shoulder more of the blame yourself. This may seem like a revelation of your weakness, but it helps others to know that you are human and less than perfect. Such deliberate vulnerability endears you to subordinates and makes the leaders above you know that you have leadership ability. Taking the least credit and accepting more blame makes you the bigger person because in that way you demonstrate humility and a rare form of self-confidence; one that is not afraid to look bad.

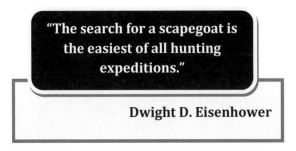

"The search for a scapegoat is the easiest of all hunting expeditions."

Dwight D. Eisenhower

Instead of scapegoating the subordinates, it is wise to spend more time coaching and training your staff to be the best, reach their deadlines and achieve their goals. When a subordinate does well, it will motivate them to hear their leader mention them and the milestone of achievement. Build the confidence of those who are struggling by creating the atmosphere for self redemption. Furthermore, where the sharing of the blame and the affirming of subordinates for success has been done, it has helped in creating economic and social value.

THE ABUSE OF POWER

The attainment to leadership brings different kinds of power; positional, informational, financial and functional power. All powers come with strings of responsibility.

The abuse of power is when someone with a degree of power over people by virtue of their dexterity, social position, physical strength, wealth, weapon, technology or the strength others repose in them, use the power unjustifiably to exploit, harm and damage others or through the lack of action allow others to cause harm.

The abuse of power is when position is used to intimidate subordinates or those who serve with the leader. #It is when subordinates are threatened or their work sabotaged because the leader has an access and opportunity that the people the leader intimidates does not have.

The first and most paramount form of abuse is when leaders become bullies. In its extreme form the bullying leader uses sarcasm, yelling, physical violence and manhandling of subordinates.

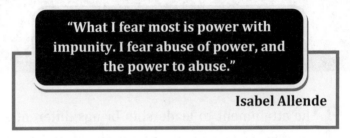

"What I fear most is power with impunity. I fear abuse of power, and the power to abuse."

Isabel Allende

In the name of performance, the bully humiliates, violates and intimidates the staff until he or she chooses to stay away from the reach of the leader.

Some other leaders use manipulation to abuse and violate their subordinates. They start by putting emphasis on a purported promotion. That promise of promotion lures the staff into long hours of work. When the time comes to make the promise good, the manipulative boss reneges, meanwhile he has achieved his desires for additional productivity or meeting a deadline. Manipulation takes other forms; keeping the people under a leader uninformed, without any mentoring or training so that no one rises above him.

DEFICIENCY IN PROBLEM SOLVING SKILLS

> "We must remember that one determined person can make a significant difference, and that a small group of determined people can change the course of history."
>
> **Sonia Johnson**

A deficiency in problem solving skills results in the exacerbation of small problems. In certain parts of the world, especially the third world, this weakness in leadership happens when politicians or local leaders believe their job is not to provide a good environment for business but to fiddle, centralize control, micro-manage and engage in self aggrandizement at the cost of the citizen's welfare.

The true depth of leadership will be exposed in the face challenges. There will be obstacles but some do not show until decisions have been made.

Enhancing your leadership through the ability to solve problems will require a few steps:

APPROACH ALL ISSUES WITH CLARITY

A high energy approach to issues will not resolved them. It might become counterproductive. Rather it would be wise to come up with a systematic, clear and logical approach, even if there is limited time to do this. This first step is like the road map to an intended destination.

GET CRACKING WITH THE ISSUES.

Once you start focusing on the problem and seeking for solutions, it is important to break down the problem, in order to get to the root of the matter. It is necessary to know the cause and the effect of the issues to develop a robust solution.

WORK OUT A PROBLEM SOLVING STRATEGY

Start with an end result in mind. See the result you want to achieve in your mind and start working towards it. The nature of the problem pre-determines the solution proffered.

EXECUTE, EXECUTE, EXECUTE

Following a planned strategy, you should now execute the plan you have conceived. There is nothing like a failproof strategy, however it would be good to approach matters with the tried and tested strategy. However, you will need to review your approach and adapt it based on the issue at hand. The execution of your strategy may bring about a change in the dynamics of the matter at hand; this should still not deter you from re-evaluating your approach.

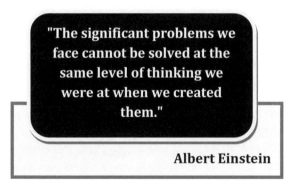

"The significant problems we face cannot be solved at the same level of thinking we were at when we created them."

Albert Einstein

CHECK YOUR RESULTS

You have designed an approach to solving problems, it is now important to evaluate the effectiveness of your approach. If the result falls below expectation, then you may need to check your approach. Was there an error in your approach? Were there perspectives to the matter which was hidden from you? Could the error be in the execution and not the approach designed? Several attempts must be made to resolve an issue, rather than give up at the slightest hint of failure. A leader must bear in mind that for problems to be solved qualitatively, his approach must be with a logical, focused and clear mind.

9

POOR COMMUNICATION SKILLS

Leadership will fail if there is an inability to properly disseminate information that is necessary for the progress of an organization. When leadership fails through bad communication it is often because of assumptions, wanting to assert rights, and the creation of negative communication patterns.

Everything a leader does, communicates; what he encodes and how he encodes it are important.

The communication must be clear, concise, concrete, correct, coherent, complete and courteous because although the leader stands and seems to be in front of everyone else; the people working with him also deserve to be shown respect. Looking at the characteristics of communication in more detail, we said ascertained that it needs to be:

CLEAR

The communicator needs to be clear on what he intends to communicate and that it is clear to him. The onus should not be on your listeners or readers to try to make sense of what you want to communicate and draw their own conclusion.

Clarity in communication is achieved when people have an assertive statement which guides them towards an intended goal.

CONCISE

Keeping it simple is the beauty of good communication. There is no need to be verbose with words if you can say it in a more precise and shorter way. It is not the length of the sentence but the ability to pack a punch in a short missive.

CONCRETE

Concrete communication is making every attempt to leave your audience with the facts. It should also be focused on the main subject.

CORRECT

There will be leadership failure if communication is laden or loaded with misinformation, misleading statements and half truths. It is a grievous error to get names, places and figures wrong. Leadership is more than standing in front of people and bellowing commands; it is making every effort to be a good example in all things.

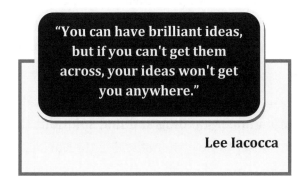

"You can have brilliant ideas, but if you can't get them across, your ideas won't get you anywhere."

Lee Iacocca

COHERENT

It is a gross error to communicate as if you are talking to people on another planet. No soldier will respond to a bugle which makes the wrong sound. Avoid text language as much as possible when writing in your capacity as a leader, because of its likely way of corrupting good communication.

COMPLETE

A complete message will have an introduction, a body and a conclusion. The body of the message should be adequate enough for the recipient to act with. Many followers have been often left to act on assumptions and perceived opinions on what they think the leader wants.

COURTEOUS

Many leaders have failed because of discourteous communication. Talking down to people reduces productivity, and demotivates them. Being courteous is to be friendly, open, warm and honest without being insulting.

The most major goal of effective communication is to create mutual understanding and find solutions that could be mutually acceptable or beneficial to the various parties.

#10

BLIND TO THE CURRENT SITUATION

Leadership fails when it buries its head in the sand like the proverbial ostrich; pretending that there are no issues or no challenges at hand until suddenly problems get to the point of no return. Successful leaders are known to make quick decisions, and once the decision is made they set to work immediately.

While commenting on an article entitled "*YarAdua and a sick nation*" by Okey Ndibe, a blogger wrote "YarAdua's friends and family ought to tell him that...Nigerians... deserve an energetic, intelligent, vibrant, and visionary leader to run their affairs". The comment refers to the late president of Nigeria who was bogged down with kidney problems, and an administration perceived to be inept, inefficient, and saddled with bungling incompetence.

Sometimes when leadership finds itself in this situation it becomes worse if it has succeeded in surrounding itself with empty praise singers.

Being inept and blind to the immediate need of people has cost cities like New Orleans, when the floods came and the government was slow to act.

It's a reminder of leaders like Emperor Nero who was busy entertaining his guests while Rome was burning.

> "The real distinction is between those who adapt their purposes to reality and those who seek to mold reality in the light of their purposes."
>
> **Henry Kissinger**

Leadership will fail unless it realizes that the first rule of winning is "don't escape from reality". In order to not get sucked into the challenge of escaping from the reality of the immediate, Jack Welch suggested in his book: *Straight From the Gut.* That successful leadership must be able to:

1.Control your destiny or someone else will

2.Face reality as it is, not as it was or as you wish it were

3.Be candid with everyone

4.Don't manage, lead

5.Change before you have to

6.If you don't have a competitive advantage, don't compete

THE DISCOURAGEMENT OF OTHERS

L eadership is meant to inspire, encourage, challenge, and provoke people to excellence. It fails when it does the opposite. It discourages others from getting involved in making things happen.

Why do leaders discourage instead of inspiring people to aspire? There may be several reasons, but the ones which seem to stand out are:

A DESIRE TO FEEL SPECIAL COMPARED TO OTHERS

Have you ever asked a successful leader how they got to where they are? The answer often starts with some impossible obstacle that they had to overcome to get to where they are. When people who have a multi-million dollar business tell us that they started with nothing, we feel inadequate and unable to match their endurance and tenacity.

TOO MUCH STRUGGLE

Some leaders overwhelm you with the statistics of the people who have failed while trying to make it in that chosen field. They reel out the percentage of people who entered that field and the high turnover of failure. Truly, only few people make it to the top in a lot of careers. But there is no evidence that the enquirer will spend as many years trying to make it as those who have gone ahead of him. It is unfair for a leader to assume that it will take others the same number of years it took him before there was a result.

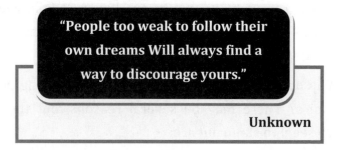

"People too weak to follow their own dreams Will always find a way to discourage yours."

Unknown

SCARCITY CONSCIOUSNESS

A third reason why many leaders discourage the up and coming is the consciousness that there might be job scarcity in that chosen field in the future. Leaders in this category see new comers as competition and therefore do all they can to discourage their 'competitors' possible entrance.

However there are people who have not only achieved leadership success, but are willing to equip others for effective leadership in the future.

> "Keep away from people who try to belittle your ambitions. Small people always do that, but the really great ones make you feel that you, too, can become great."
>
> **Mark Twain**

12

A KNOW-IT-ALL ATTITUDE

Weak leadership sometimes covers up its ignorance by putting on a know-it-all attitude pretending to have all the answers when it has absolutely none.

A know-it-all attitude makes the leader less caring. It also makes it difficult for a person to be true to the very attributes that made them successful. You might ask how this could be possible; well, the fact is that the very source of a leader's power can also be what draws him into this negative behaviour.

KNOWLEDGE POWER

This represents a leader's talent, education, wisdom, abilities and skills. This power resulted in quick elevation for many. However, if left unchecked, it also makes the leader develop a know-it-all attitude. In this frame of mind the failing leader refuses to acknowledge other sources, does not know the subordinates very well, and claims expertise in areas that are a blind spot for him.

ATTRACTION POWER

This is the ability to draw people to yourself because of your warmth, wisdom, physical or charismatic attraction. It easily gets a leader national and global influence and effectiveness. However, this can turn against the leader when he becomes moody, aloof, arrogant and self absorbed.

EXPRESSIVE POWER

Many have attained to positions of repute because of their oratorical and communicative skills. The power of eloquence through writing, speaking and poetry really increases a leader's influence more than most other sources. However, when the leader begins to have a know-it-all attitude, they talk too much and listen less.

CREDIBILITY POWER

A man's reputation power is drawn from how he is perceived in the community, at work, business and society at large. This power source undergirds and brings greater value to the leader. It also requires a lot of protection.

When an arrogant feeling gives the leader the belief that he is larger than life and doesn't need to give due consideration to the impact of his choices and associations; and that he can go free for almost anything he does; leadership failure becomes inevitable.

Leadership must be viewed as a first among equal standpoint not a superior, above the inferior, otherwise a know-it-all attitude will manifest and destroy the effect leadership ought to have. Breaking from this tendency will require an exposure to a variety of ideas, people, and opinions. It is important that you act, or else you will choke your own success.

> "The only fool bigger than the person who knows it all is the person who argues with him"
>
> **Stanislaw Jerzy Lec**

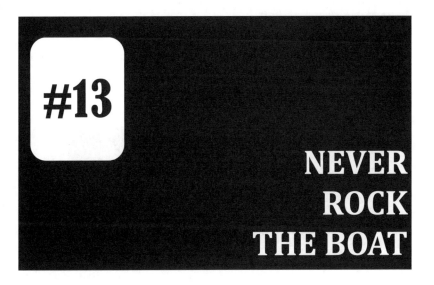

#13

NEVER
ROCK
THE BOAT

F ailure is inevitable when leadership settles for the regular and the mundane.

The concept of rocking the boat comes from the idea of the impact a team of people rowing a boat can make. If each occupant rows at a different speed there is the possibility that the boat will be rocked.

Rocking the boat to some people who like things steady and continuous could be perceived as causing trouble or disturbance within a group. This language is used especially when you try to bring a change to a situation that most people think does not need a change.

Steps towards overcoming this tendency must begin with a deliberate desire to:

Rebuke yourself and colleagues from comfort zones.

Success has a way of sucking you into the zone of over celebrating past achievements. Progress is possible as you continue to challenge yourself.

> "The person who risks nothing, does nothing, has nothing, is nothing, and becomes nothing. He may avoid suffering and sorrow, but he simply cannot learn and feel and change and grow and love and live."
>
> **Leo F. Buscaglia**

Rock the boat by constantly challenging yourself to grow. It is important to raise the bar if you must avoid complacency.

Rocking the boat also suggests taking risks, doing things which look crazy to those who like the predictable life.

Innovate. Stability is good for business, but the demands on leadership of the 21st century is to push the boundaries and do something new. Innovation in this context is either the birthing of a new idea or a wholesome re-invention of what can put your organization in front and be of value to your customers.

Augment. Take new ideas and run wild with them.

Consolidate. Once you step out with an innovation that

will change things in an organization, you will need to consolidate the grounds you have gained so that there is no reversal to the status quo. This can be achieved as you consolidate power, processes, and systems. These actions will help to break the cycle of pulling the wagons of leadership in a circle.

So many leaders have refused to proffer change because of the fear of being perceived as a trouble maker. However if things are not disrupted, if things are done in the name of harmony - even when it is apparent to everyone that there is need for a change - leadership will end up failing.

#14

SABOTAGING THE SUCCESS OF OTHER PEOPLE

S abotage is a deliberate act carried out to destroy, obstruct or hinder other persons.

It is a wilful destruction undermining, countermining or counteracting the good deeds of other people in order to make them look bad.

It sounds ludicrous that a leader will work towards the sabotage of his own team, but this happens. Some of the cases are deliberate while others are actions which end up spelling out sabotage on the part of the leader towards his direct reports or team members. Let us examine actions which are tantamount to sabotage. Some of them have been mentioned under other reasons for leadership failure:

INCORRECT DIAGNOSIS OF PROBLEMS

Failing leaders have a habit of putting the blame for under-performance and high staff turnover at the doorstep of lazy or bad employees. High staff turnover is often because of the poor management style of the leader.

PROJECTING A NEGATIVE VISION

Vision is the tool for propelling an organization forward. It is projected to the followership in three ways; positive vision, maintaining status quo, or a negative outlook. The success of the organization and the people will be sabotaged if the leader becomes negative about the future of the organization. It is very hard to be successful in an atmosphere where you are told tomorrow will be worse than today.

DISRESPECTFUL COMMUNICATION

Words have power. They can convey vision and make demotivated people feel like they are alive again. Conversely, people feel deflated when the leader uses foul language, barks orders, threatens or speaks in a condescending manner.

WITHHOLDING RECOGNITION

It is easy for squeaky wheels to get the most attention. Failing leaders sabotage their people by overlooking conscientious and hard working staff while they complain when there are mistakes. People need to know what they are doing well, so they can be better at it.

DISPLAYING CONFLICTING VALUES

Acting in a way that conflicts with the values the leader purports to hold impacts the followership in a negative way and sabotages their success. People tend to affirm the behaviours they observe.

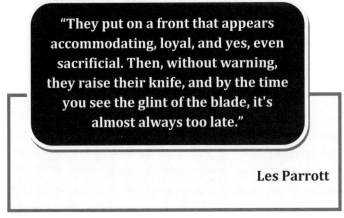

"They put on a front that appears accommodating, loyal, and yes, even sacrificial. Then, without warning, they raise their knife, and by the time you see the glint of the blade, it's almost always too late."

Les Parrott

STAYING ON

Imagine a leader who has lost hope in the future of the organization where he is supposed to be part of. He no longer believes in the department he heads, and takes delight in telling everyone how the place is hopeless. The irony of it is that he never resigns or moves away. Instead of inspiring vision and helping to raise great leaders of the future, he becomes toxic and pollutes other minds.

When a leader takes this view or angle, he has failed in his responsibility.

Using a method which subverts and weakens those who serve under us or with us is not a proof of strength or quality leadership; it is proof that leadership has failed.

#15

GETTING OTHERS TO DO WHAT THEY ARE UNWILLING TO DO

The basic meaning of leading is to show the way by going ahead in advance to guide or direct in a chorus. Leading is to serve as a route for others to take; to be the channel or conduit others see and feel inspired to follow.

There are various reasons why being the example and the first to do things is a way to enhance leadership:

People need a sample. People always need someone they can benchmark against. A lack of example leaves people confused and dissuades them from following.

People need to be challenged to confidence. Organizations pontificate on the need for achieving goals but they fail to realize the power of leading by example. It is easier to build confidence and follow a leader who does things first before asking others to do so.

If the leader does not do it, nobody will. It is an utter misconception to come up with a vision and simply expect it to be implemented by others. If you do not initiate the implementation, the chances of it being carried out are zero.

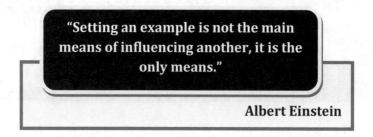

> "Setting an example is not the main means of influencing another, it is the only means."
>
> **Albert Einstein**

The leader must start it or it will never be started. Setting the standards and rules as a leader is not enough. The implementation is best if the leader who set the rules also sets the standard for best practice.

True leaders are followed because they create the pathway, and become pathfinders on matters which others have never attempted before. They become the beacon of light to help others out of their ignorance and darkness.

When a leader fails to show which way to do a thing but rather only tells people what to do, there will be leadership failure.

16

DICTATORIAL LEADERSHIP: INTIMIDATING, THREATENING AND USING ULTIMATUMS

> "It is a paradox that every dictator has climbed to power on the ladder of free speech. Immediately on attaining power each dictator has suppressed all free speech except his own."
>
> **Herbert Hoover**

The use of the word dictatorship brings images of leaders like; Hitler, Saddam Hussein, Josef Stalin or Fidel Castro to our minds.

How do you know if a leader is turning into a dictator? By the brute force he uses to motivate.

Firstly, he solicits, secures and uses his absolute power. Absolute power they say corrupts absolutely.

Secondly, dictators promote genocide. In other words, the destruction of as many or almost all people as long as their desire is established.

The aforementioned were known to have made chemicals for the destruction of people, including those whom they governed.

Thirdly, they like to create an atmosphere of group affirmation. It is either everyone dressing the way they want as in the case of Saddam Hussein where almost everyone in the republican army had a certain type of moustache. In Hitler's day everyone wore a brown shirt; in the days of Mussolini everyone wore a black shirt.

In North Korea, when people laughed they laughed en mass and when they cried, particularly at the loss of their dictatorial leader, there was mass weeping.

Dictators are also essentially eccentric; however the final words on the lips of a dictator is *ME   ME   ME*. They have the characteristic of being egocentric.

#17

THEY DO NOT LISTEN FOR FEEDBACK FROM THE FOLLOWERSHIP

L eadership fails when it fails to seek feedback; when it refuses to seek and receive feedback.

> "The ear of the leader must ring with the voices of the people."
>
> **Woodrow Wilson**

Feedback is input on our work, it could be as simple as a short verbal comment that makes us know what is going on. Feedback will help the leader know if he is achieving his goal, will help him know if he is truly on course, and it will help him know if the followership understands his role as leader.

Finally, it will give the leader an understanding if he is making the appropriate impact.

To serve or lead without feedback is to seem as if you are on an important journey without a map or signpost, and when you are being warned that you are off course, you ignore all the warning signs. Leadership will fail with such an attitude.

The most appropriate thing to do is to ask questions, such as:

☐   Why am I a leader?

☐   What am I supposed to achieve?

☐   How is my performance tracking?

☐   What is the best use of my time?

☐   How am I influencing others?

☐   What is the quality of my relationship with the followership?

☐   How am I serving my team members?

#18

THEY AVOID DIFFERENT OPINIONS

Holding different opinions or potential conflict does not make them go away. Sometimes a difference of opinion can highlight a view the leader may not have considered and this could be important for the progress of the organization.

> "It is not best that we should all think alike; it is a difference of opinion that makes horse races."
>
> **Mark Twain**

Leaders who are unable to hear a different opinion have set themselves in motion for failure.

To improve a situation, there must be a change from an

attitude of US against THEM to a situation where the leader establishes a "WE" mindset that will allow him to embrace new or shared perspectives.

Furthermore, in order to avoid the action that leads to failure, a leader can identify an alignment in the values he and the people he leads holds, to forestall a situation where he is being perceived as avoiding a difference of opinion.

A leader can ask questions like *"how do we want to treat each other during our conversations on this matter?"* and *"how can we find out what values our opinions will create?"* Rather than taking sides in an argument that may end up being futile and unfruitful.

#19

FUZZY VISION

Have you ever looked through a lens or camera when it is not well focused? The image appears fuzzy and if the picture is taken the image will most likely be fuzzy too.

The leader whose vision and perspective of the future is unclear will lead his people to the realms of failure. Clarity is what allows one to communicate visions effectively, without it, it is hard to answer even the most basic questions about what you are out to achieve and why.

A fuzzy vision makes you unable to answer what your business is out to do and why you are in business. A fuzzy vision means you cannot precisely articulate where you are going, nor can you persuade your customers, partners or investors to believe in what you are doing. When this is the case, leadership fails.

It is important to be able to effectively communicate vision. What distinguishes failed leaders and effective ones is that magnetic quality in successful leaders that enables them to effectively communicate their vision.

When the vision of the leader is clear, and communicated to the organization, it facilitates the atmosphere for success.

a. A clear vision will help the people to embrace change and adapt their jobs accordingly

b. In an atmosphere where the vision is made plain by the leader, the workers are able to discuss issues openly.

c. The morale of the people involved with the leader is high, while the staff turnover is low.

d. The measurement of performance is based on the team spirit and not mere individual drive.

Fuzzy leadership paralyses progress, and causes issues to be swept under the carpet for fear of conflict and arguments.

Kodak, the photography company, went digital in the 80s and became a phenomenal success. However its attempt to give a huge part of its re-organization over to a new management system made its original vision unfocused. . The end result was a disaster; Kodak is right now in receivership; having declared itself bankrupt. It is unimaginable that a business with an annual turnover of $20 billion could head for such a disaster.

#20

LACK OF LEADERSHIP SKILLS

In his book *Twelfth Knight*, Shakespeare said: "*some are born great, some achieve greatness and some have greatness thrust upon them.*"

True as this may be, it could be the reason why many people fail in leadership particularly where greatness or leadership, is thrust upon them.

People assume leadership of nations by default because they occupy certain roles in the political party that is in the majority. So, leadership becomes a functional opportunity; for others it is a mere position.

A person who finds himself occupying a position of leadership as a function or opportunity thrust upon them, may not have come to that post with the skill that is necessary to make it a success.

The irony for failure in leadership is that while all leaders have the ability to manage, only a small proportion of people who are managers have the necessary skills to become strong leaders. This inability stifles business and results in failure because the person who is most likely to climb the ladder of leadership is the one who has grown through the ranks.

> "If the blind lead the blind, both shall fall in the ditch."
>
> **Jesus Christ**

#21

DISCOURAGING CULTURE

Leadership fails when the person at the helm of affairs, along with the system they operate in becomes bogged down in corporate cultures that do not inspire.

They fail when there are no shared values and employees are not energized. They are bogged down in the culture of blame and they do not celebrate diversity.

> "With time and patience, the mulberry leaf becomes satin. With time and patience the mulberry leaf becomes a silk gown."
>
> **Chinese Proverb**

22

LACK OF INITIATIVE

> "Success depends in a very large measure upon individual initiative and exertion, and cannot be achieved except by a dint of hard work."

Anna Pavlova

Taking the initiative is a fundamental leadership qualification and an indicator of competence. You will stand out if you do not merely settle for the regular way of doing things, but think outside of the box and ask questions like "why not?" when others are asking "why?" True leaders choose their work; the work does not choose them. Such people settle for the work they like, where they can distinguish themselves. If the work is not forthcoming, leaders with initiative create it.

Taking the initiative will mean selecting and influencing the place in which you work, rather than reacting to situations created by others.

The leader with initiative works to change their circumstances and themselves for the better.

True leaders will create a vision, set the goals that will make the vision possible and inspire the action that will lead to the fulfilment of the vision.

It means operating beyond comfort zones and setting "stretch" goals that will enable the leader and his co-workers develop new skills.

Leaders must build a lot of self confidence. Without it you will be afraid of the negative feedback from those who disagree with your actions and decisions.

Take the initiative by responding quickly to the opportunities spotted by your colleagues, and or the observations of your customers.

Leaders will initiate the use of their organization's core competence to bring solutions to new clients.

Use your initiative as a leader to analyze your ideas before presenting it to others. Do a cost/benefit analysis. Check out the risk and impact analysis before others do.

Taking the initiative has several benefits among which are: improved products and services, a lot of enhancement for the organization and the job, the job is made easier and better and increasing the chances of success for individuals and the corporate body.

Leadership with initiative is an absolute necessity for progress. If imitative is missing, the employees or followers are not empowered; there is poor motivation. The people end up feeling as though their contribution is unnecessary. This is a mark of leadership that is doomed to fail.

One of the things which marks out a leader as separate from the manager is the ability to initiate or innovate. Managers tend to maintain the status quo.

Leadership fails when it is unable to initiate a dream, a vision, or a project that will move the organization forward.

> "There are three types of people in this world: those who make things happen, those who watch things happen, and those who wonder what happened."
>
> **Mary Kay Ash**

#23

HIGH BUREAUCRACY

Many organizations discourage creative thinking; they create so many layers of challenges and approval methods; as a result those who want to move the organization forward feel discouraged. The system which was designed to help the organization achieve, ends up being the broken cog in its own wheel.

An organization is considered bureaucratic, when its customers or target market perceive that its services are enveloped in red tape. The policies are inflexible and no longer satisfy the customers. Everyone is made to fit in the same box and treated alike. This may be because everyone is just a number and are not treated as individuals.

At its highest level, bureaucracy foments political infighting, with executives striving for personal power and advancement. It makes various departments fail to cooperate with other departments, and in some cases ideas are killed because they come from "the wrong person"; while the same idea would be supported if it were from "the right person".

In highly bureaucratic settings, leaders hoard information and use it as a source of power. If information is released, it is used selectively or distorted to make a failing leader's department look better.

In this setting, mistakes are denied, covered up or hidden. Failing leaders play the blame game, shifting their errors on other people. The popular aspect of bureaucracy which is known the world over is how larger and larger number of people make decisions, this means that no one is really held responsible for the decision or the outcome

When a leader is high on bureaucracy and low on vision; leadership is bound to fail.

Preventing failure for the organization and the leader is possible. This will be as the leader:

SEEKS PROFESSIONAL HELP

External people are good when you want to initiate change. Subsequently the new approach will have to be owned by the people in the system in order to be effective.

STRIVES FOR CONTINUOUS IMPROVEMENT

The use of continuous improvement, as opposed to a traditional managerial system will multiply the amount of change and enhance the quality of output of the organization. A commitment to improvement will make the company attract new blood and trigger the reduction or removal of bureaucracy.

ENVISIONS THE FUTURE

Paint a picture of the desired future for the organization and begin to work towards it. Making the change possible may require consulting widely with the stakeholders; customers and management.

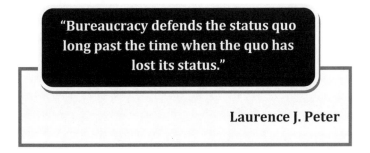

"Bureaucracy defends the status quo long past the time when the quo has lost its status."

Laurence J. Peter

24

POOR KNOWLEDGE MANAGEMENT

The topography of business corporations, countries and organizations has changed because of the availability of knowledge. However, this knowledge needs to be properly harnessed and managed.

Knowledge management is that discipline which enables teams, and entire organizations, to collectively and systematically share, create and apply knowledge to enable a better achievement of goals. It is a necessary part of today's leadership because it is no use doing the same thing every day without capturing and distributing the knowledge gained. The following should be considered:

a. Making knowledge management worthwhile requires knowing what information needs to be managed and for what performance end.

b. It would mean capturing information which is necessary for the progress of the organization and making it available for use. This allows everyone in the system to access the appropriate information.

c. Bring the people, processes, work culture and the enabling technology together, to achieve a wholesome avenue of knowledge.

Several factors seem to be driving the need to manage knowledge, paramount among them is the fact that today's work environment is becoming increasingly complex and saddled with issues that have never been dealt with before.

Knowledge management is also necessary because of the tendency for middle and top management to operate without applying knowledge management.

He who has the appropriate, current and most relevant information will always be in front. However it is not enough to have information it is important to be able to capture and transfer this knowledge and prevent its loss.

One telephone conversation could mean the transferring of information that could potentially provide multi-millions for a company.

Good leaders of the 21st century will create a knowledge base for creative ideas and a system for managing the knowledge, ideas and strategies that are generated so that it is not stolen or misused.

When leadership lacks or fails in its capacity or ability to do this, then leadership has failed.

> "Information is a source of learning. But unless it is organized, processed, and available to the right people in a format for decision making, it is a burden, not a benefit."
>
> **William Pollard**

#25

POOR TEAMWORK

"Conflict is inevitable in a team ... in fact, to achieve synergistic solutions, a variety of ideas and approaches are needed. These are the ingredients for conflict."

Susan Gerke

There are several styles of leadership including:

- [ ] Transactional
- [ ] Transformational
- [ ] Autocratic
- [ ] Laissez faire
- [ ] Free rein
- [ ] Charismatic

Whatever method a leader chooses to adopt, it must go hand in hand with a commitment to team work. When a team has not been able to operate effectively after it has been formed; it still comes down to the quality of leadership at the helm of leading this team.

Signs of bad teamwork are friction and disagreements, falling behind on deadlines, an inability to meet targets, and focusing attention and energy on other objectives.

Teamwork suffers when complaints and gossip from various sources are heard by team members. However, this will not have a great impact if the leadership is strong but Where there is poor leadership, rules will be unclear, the goals of the team will be unclear, training will be inadequate, there will be differences in work style and poor planning. When all this happens, leadership has failed.

#26

FAILING LEADERS CREATE A SYSTEM OF CONFUSION

> "Order is never observed; it is disorder that attracts attention because it is awkward and intrusive."
>
> **Eliphas Levi**

When this happens, in the end the left does not know what the right is doing. It is interesting to note that in certain cases the atmosphere of confusion and chaos deliberately created by the leadership in order to control everyone and have the final say. When this happens leadership still has failed.

27

POOR CROSS-FUNCTIONAL COLLABORATION

As organizations grow, functions become multiple and as this happens it becomes necessary to know how to synchronize the various functions and create a wholesome atmosphere of success. The world in which we live is now complex. Nothing seems as it used to, such complexity requires the application of a wide range of approaches, skills, ideas and perspectives.

The skill to manage a multiple level organization is a determining factor for a manager. For example, when transitioning from managing a segment of a business to carrying differing opinions, teams, and people along.

The old functional method centralized power, knowledge and skill in the manager or leader. Hierarchy and superiority on the basis of age or year of service is still holding many organizations back from maximizing opportunities.

To avoid leadership failure, a step in the right direction would be to form cross management teams, drawn from the various departments, e.g. Engineering, Research, Marketing, Finance and Human Resources. They would be responsible for:

a. Social collaboration and the creation of concepts

b. The creation of new designs and products for the organisation

c. The team helps the transitions needed. i.e. technology

d. The team collaborates to control the cost of production and improve the profit level

The formation of a team is no guarantee of success. The potential members need to have the required skill for reform, the political connection and the will to carry through the charter. They must also be able to work together. The ability to work together would sometimes be predicated upon, the ground rules agreed.

That as it may, throwing people together from various departments may not achieve the collaboration desired, an effective team would have to be the function of effective training and preparation.

You can only move the organization forward by developing a mindset which carries everyone along; the creation of a cross functional management committee.

"It is the long history of humankind (and animal kind, too) those who learned to collaborate and improvise most effectively have prevailed."

Charles Darwin

#28

GREED

G reed manifests as an insatiable desire for control, manipulation and domination.

Powerful leaders have often been seen to find ways to do what seems to be in their own best interest rather than the common good. This has no other name than greed.

Greed is the selfish pursuit of money, wealth, power or possession especially when this denies the same goods to others. This pursuit is beyond what an individual needs and becomes an imbalance to other needs.

Greed in leadership is the reason why a leader pays crumbs to workers and still feels that his dog should earn better.

Greed can manifest in different ways; exploiting workers to reap management rewards is greed in leadership. When a leader is working for greedy self interest, he finds it hard to work with a greater vision that would bring a change to those he leads.

Greed makes a poor leader say: *"I am going to get mine, since everyone else is and besides I deserve it".* In effect, greedy leadership stinks whether it is on **Wall Street** or **Broad Street**.

A leader who does not want to fail through this particular monster will have to create an atmosphere for intense oversight and accountability. Greed was at the root of the challenges of the Enron Corporation and WorldCom incorporated, where **Bernie Ebbers** was knee deep in fraud and deception. The same goes for **Dennis Kozlowski** former CEO of Tyco International Limited.

> **"Greed is the inventor of injustice as well as the current enforcer."**
>
> **Julian Casablancas**

#29

THE EAGERNESS TO PLEASE

This cause of failure in leadership stems from the previous subject dealt with; a sense of insecurity. It makes such a leader to want to win because they see their service or cause as a popularity contest. If there is no one to contest with they seem to do it with their own alter ego.

The desire to please people makes a leader miss out on pleasing the right people. The chief reason for trying to please is the strong desire for approval. It all begins with the childhood setting, where the compliance with the wishes and desires of others has created an addiction for approval. They become what they think other people want them to be.

Once they grow into adulthood the habit continues with dozens of variations. At its most extreme the people pleaser becomes a 'doormat' or pushover. Ironically, being a pushover gives them the feeling of security and alleviates their social insecurities.

Leadership failure is inevitable with this tendency because it tends to make the leader spineless. An uncontrolled eagerness to please will lead to loss of integrity, identity, self respect, self esteem and could result in self belittling.

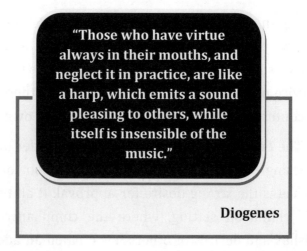

"Those who have virtue always in their mouths, and neglect it in practice, are like a harp, which emits a sound pleasing to others, while itself is insensible of the music."

Diogenes

HOW DO YOU BREAK FREE FROM THE PEOPLE PLEASING SYNDROME?

The first step is to know how to say No without feeling guilty

What is the use of having the entire relations of your spouse in your home at Christmas, when it makes you unhappy?

Set boundaries

What do you consider to be the farthest a person can go before you say no? accepting the unacceptable, making the abnormal look normal, and tolerating the intolerable will make people push the boundaries you set and violate you. Label the actions you consider unacceptable and set the limits on people's behaviour.

You have a choice

Never leave yourself without a choice. Part of that choice is the ability to turn down some requests.

Do not be manipulated

It is important to watch out for manipulators and those who flatter. Flatterers will deliberately praise you, so that you will be obliged to please them. Before you know it, you are either deciding to please them, or they make decisions for you.

Be emphatic

Make sure you are heard and understood to be saying no to what will please others and displease you.

Empty apologies

People pleasers have a habit for apologizing for what they do not seem to be guilty of. The leader needs to truly ask himself if he was responsible for any wrong. If the answer is no, do not apologise.

#30 PERFECTIONISM

Perfectionism becomes a reason for leadership failure because it makes the individual focus on things to the point of micro managing. It is not to be mistaken for being perfect or doing things perfectly, rather it involves putting oneself under pressure to meet high standards, which then powerfully influences the way we think about ourselves.

Perfectionism may mean focusing so much attention on things that do not have a major consequence when it comes to the total vision of the leader.

Perfectionism is a relentless travel for extremely high standards, even when they are almost unattainable. It is judging yourself largely on your ability to achieve an unachievable standard.

Perfectionism may be demanding standards and continuing to pursue them even if the cost is huge emotionally, financially, physically and relationally.

Though few people will assume or agree that they are perfectionists they may say things like:

- ☐ *"I like being very organized, very efficient"*

- ☐ *"I like being prepared for every event and get satisfaction in knowing that I have tried my hardest, it makes me feel special"*

- ☐ *"I like to do things very well"*

- ☐ *"I get pleasure from achieving things that others cannot do"*

The paradox of perfectionism is that while the leader is focused on trying to do things excellently, they create an atmosphere for those who work with them that is unhealthy, unhelpful and often times in the end misses the main matter.

It brings to mind the story of the captain and his co-pilot who were about to land a plane and because one little button would not work, they both gave it their fullest attention even though it would not have stopped the plane from landing. They were so focused on the button and never knew that they were about to crash; by the time they realized it was too late.

> "But I am learning that perfection isn't what matters. In fact, it's the very thing that can destroy you if you let it."
>
> **Emily Giffin**

#31

ARROGANCE

A rrogant leadership is about those who believe they are superior to everyone else. It may not be said in words but the actions of the leader who sets himself up for failure says they he is right and everyone else is wrong. It is a delusional belief that they are better than anyone else.

Leadership arrogance is not self confidence, self confidence manifests in the way you carry yourself; in your interactions and actions. Arrogance exceeds self confidence; it is the belief of an arrogant leader that because of his talent, ideas and results he is superior to everyone else.

While self-confidence is necessary for leadership success, arrogance is a danger because it alienates staff, it constricts your success and it negates your impact.

Arrogant people tell others what they want to hear; humble people serve higher purposes. Humble leaders put organizational success before their own. Arrogant leaders put their own success before the organization.

Arrogant leaders emphasis their responsibilities; they don't have time for people, they have time for themselves. Arrogant leaders are more focused on what they will get than on what they will give. They are more focused on who serves them, than on who they serve.

Arrogant leaders brag about themselves; they blame everyone around them instead of taking responsibility

> "Love measures our stature: the more we love, the bigger we are. There is no smaller package in all the world than that of a man all wrapped up in himself."
>
> **William Sloane Coffin**

#32

POWER

The use of power is one of the most delicate subjects when it comes to success or failure of leadership. In best practice, it can be used judiciously and for worthy goals. However, when it goes wrong it can be abused and used to hurt the followership. Either way, leaders must understand the power they possess.

The appropriate use of power will motivate, challenge, provoke and even raise new leaders. When power is used to dominate people in order to get the job done, leadership has failed. When a leader has to use physical violence including throwing things or hitting people, then leadership has gone wrong.

Then there is the abuser of power. This person uses power to manipulate through psychological control of peoples' minds. This is done by making false promises and making claims that cannot be substantiated.

This may be the context in which **Lord Acton** said: *"Power tends to corrupt and absolute power corrupts absolutely."*

In most organizations, there are two strands of power; ***Position Power*** and ***Personal Power.***

Leaders have position power given to them by virtue of the organization they lead. Personal power is about the degree of influence the individual has or has been given by the followership.

That is why you may have a President of a corporation, organization or country who has positional power but lacks personal power. The abuse of power begins where a person has positional power but lacks personal power and has to make up for it. This results in shouting, screaming, making unreasonable demands, being a time thief of the staff, acting in a manner that is intimidating or setting unreasonably high levels of expectation. When a leader slips into this behaviour it may not even be the power that has corrupted them but the fear of losing power.

> "It is a mistake, that a lust for power is the mark of a great mind; for even the weakest have been captivated by it; and for minds of the highest order, it has no charms."
>
> **Charles Caleb Colton**

#33

ALOOFNESS

Aloofness causes failure in leadership because it makes the individual behave in a distant manner, physically or emotionally. It gives the impression that such a person, particularly a leader, is cold, uninterested and appears to be above the fray.

It is hard to lead with such a tendency because among many manifestations, an aloof person has mood swings and self condemning tendencies when things go wrong. This can be accompanied by frequent sadness, loneliness or resentment. Their behaviour is a thing of concern for their mentors, family members and sometimes their protégés.

In all, aloof people tend to engage in what will reduce their social interactions. They are the types of people who keep acquiring degrees, stay glued to their computer, or are excessive bookworms. They swing between being stone-cold emotionally to being intensely angry.

Why do leaders become aloof?

The behaviours people exhibit are formed over a lifetime, the position they attain does not take away the past. As a matter of fact previous experience tends to poke into the future. Leaders tend to be aloof because of:

a. Shameful experiences of the past that may have left the leader with a degree of emotional damage.

b. Fitting poorly into the family in which the leader was brought up.

c. The leader may have been publicly embarrassed for a previous poor performance.

d. Unexpected changes in the family life can cause disruption to his approach.

e. A highly competitive, critical or hostile environment may be difficult for some people to handle. Some leaders lose their nerve and confidence at such times.

f. There is the leader who is withdrawn, avoidant, and excessively reactive. There will be leadership failure if the tendency of such leaders persists.

g. Aloofness is also a product of a very controlled childhood. Some grew in the atmosphere of frequent parental criticism and deliberate embarrassment as a way of enforcing obedience and excessive parental control.

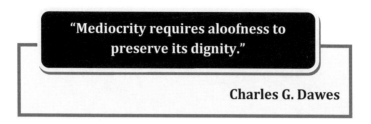

"Mediocrity requires aloofness to preserve its dignity."

Charles G. Dawes

Leaders who are aloof give the impression that they are indifferent to everybody's needs. It is very hard to lead people if you lack passion and show dullness or cluelessness. If you are emotionless or half hearted you may win by a popular vote but once you show aloofness you have separated yourself from the very people who you are supposed to carry along with you. Those whom you are meant to take to the picture you painted before them.

#34

PARANOIA

Leadership fails when it becomes paranoid. This negative tendency is expressed in different ways.

Some leaders become so paranoid that they believe bad things will always happen; it is just a matter of time. They believe it's not a matter of IF, it's a matter of WHEN.

This tendency is not only found with new leaders, sometimes high performing leaders are always thinking 'what if the negative happens'. They think about and anticipate the days of bad things. This feeling makes the leader brood over an eventuality that may never happen, or that is not even in sight.

It is not only about an event, paranoid leaders never trust anyone, they do not believe there is any such thing as loyalty. They anticipate that even the closest and most loyal will one day become disloyal. This tendency makes the leader the devil's advocate; always rolling out a negative to confront the positive and major things they are doing. Paranoia in leadership can tilt a good leader to the point of no return and make their *"what ifs"* become a major trap that make them go off the rails.

> "This is a do-it-yourself test for paranoia: you know you've got it when you can't think of anything that's your fault."
>
> **Robert M. Hutchins**

Paranoia is the dark side of the leader; it can push him over the wall and set him up for errors of judgement. Paranoia makes you suspicious of your own staff, and creates imaginary enemies. Paranoid leaders are also often in denial, never admitting failures or mistakes. A good example of this tendency was Richard Nixon; he fought imaginary enemies all of his life. He kept himself busy gathering a dossier on his supposed enemies. It was one of his paranoid pursuits of his enemies that led to the notorious Watergate scandal.

Paranoid leaders also suffer from pathological jealousy. It is hard for them to see a colleague or associate receive the accolade or appreciation. They feel that such a subordinate is there to outshine them, undermine their leadership and take away their glory. This tends to prompt them to start a process or put a system in place to checkmate their supposedly popular subordinate or associate.

For the paranoid leader, everything you do or say has a connotation, you are left with no choice but to pick your words and tiptoe around them. They run their organization with an iron fist, demanding ultimate loyalty, and running extraordinary meetings to ensure everyone is towing their line.

#35

NARCISSISM

The interesting truth is that people who are paranoid and a narcissist are common in leadership teams, and they often come as the ones ahead of the pack.

At the root of the narcissistic attitude or complex is a feeling of inferiority. However a person exhibiting this behaviour will actually present a superior attitude in order to make other people believe that through their actions and pretence, they are superior to everyone.

Narcissus is the man in Greek mythology who goes to the well and falls in love with the image he saw in the water. It was actually his own face in the reflection.

Narcissist leaders have a notion of grandeur and self importance; they are perpetually in need of admiration while on the other hand they show no sympathy or empathy for others. They overestimate their own abilities and inflict the tales of whatever they have accomplished on others.

In certain settings they are title seekers; perpetually requesting for more of them to be given.

What makes this kind of leader end up failing people is that it is not possible to maintain his narcissistic behaviour without finding co-dependents who perpetually feed his ego. He therefore raises a form of followership not leadership, who provide him with the cravings of his ego.

Leadership goes wrong when, like the naked emperor, the narcissist expects everyone to tell him that he is well dressed.

> "The sadistic narcissist perceives himself as Godlike, ruthless and devoid of scruples, capricious and unfathomable, emotion-less and non-sexual, omniscient, omnipotent and omni-present, a plague, a devastation, an inescapable verdict."
>
> **Sam Vaknin**

36

MELODRAMA

Next to the attitude of narcissism is melodrama, a cartel which results in leadership failure.

Melodramatic leaders always grab the centre of attention. Most leaders who have this tendency exhibit obvious behaviour's that suggest they are on the path to failure.

Some of the tendencies that are exhibited by them are a lack of focus. The lack of focus is the beginning of failure. While a melodramatic leader can be engaging and outgoing and interpersonally skilful; they are often unable to keep their focus.

Melodramatic leaders are also unable to perform the very act of leadership that makes a leader stand out; that is the developing of other people.

Instead of getting everyone to be focused on the objective of the organization they make their own manners and tendencies everyone's focus. In the end their subordinates feel unwanted and unneeded.

The possible leader who fits this picture would be the late Muhammad Gaddafi; he had tendencies of being unpredictable and whenever he gave a speech it could turn into non-stop ranting that went on for two to four hours.

> "The constraints of melodrama can be a great blessing, because they demand that all the characters involved - as absurd and extreme as they may initially seem - must stay utterly rooted in their own reality, or the whole project collapses."
>
> **Stanley Tucci**

In the end he attracted people to his particular style, they served his ego and helped to perpetuate his behaviour. Muhammad Gaddafi also had expectations that were highfalutin and almost unachievable. He dreamt of a united state of Africa – with himself as its leader.

People could not understand why his closest body guards were a group of female beauties. This was all part of his melodramatic scheme. Gaddafi showed up at the United Nations to make his speech, he took the constitution of the United Nations and tore it to shreds in front of everyone. Another melodramatic gesture.

A sudden turnaround of Gaddafi was his warming up to the West; it made the world seem to think that he had changed and was now ready to work with everyone. He never snapped out of his melodramatic approach; if it led to failure or not history has all that to prove.

#37

MANIC BEHAVIOUR

One of the most deadly reasons why leaders fail is manic ˌbehaviour. This is the tendency of the leaders who are obsessively driven to obtain results and in the end crash very badly.

Manic behaviour manifests as hyperactivity, increased energy and heightened mood and when it is left untreated, people's judgement become impaired resulting in reckless and dangerous behaviour.

They tend to believe that they can always make a comeback; that they are larger than life and can achieve almost anything they set their minds to. Overwhelming confusion replaces clarity and they stop keeping up with what they promise to achieve.

Manic behaviour at its most extreme alienates people and makes friends become frightened. It makes the person who is in this state become irritable, angry, frightened, uncontrollable and trapped in their uncommon drive. Such a leader goes after such thrill seeking activities that they exhibit risky behaviour until they suddenly crash. When leadership takes this turn, it is doomed for failure.

> "I still have highs and lows, just like any other person. What's missing is the lack of control over the super highs, which became destructive, and the super lows, which are immediately destructive."
>
> **Patty Duke**

#38

HAVING NO MEASURABLE OBJECTIVE

Leadership fails in this context when the leader paints a picture of an Eldorado without specific measureable milestones.

From accounting to human resources, from the man on the shop floor to the management working with the leader; everyone is in confusion because there is no way to measure if they are on course.

This kind of leader is fond of telling his staff that they will be rewarded if they achieve the objective of the organization. However, everyone is in confusion as to what the objective is.

In this context, it becomes difficult to motivate people when they do not know whether they are going in the right direction, doing well or not. Wherever there is no way of quantifying the objectives of the organization, it will result in leadership failure.

Averting failure will mean that the leader develops a working plan:

a. The plan will have time management at its foundation; a man who cannot manage time will have difficulty managing a life or lives.

b. He prioritizes tasks within his team and ensures that the company or organization's objective is carried out.

c. Focusing on the objectives of the organization, the leader prioritizes the tasks given to the team members.

d. Meeting objectives also requires that a leader knows how to allocate resources to the objectives and stays close to monitor outcomes.

e. Leadership will be effective if the future is predicated upon a clearly defined and detailed business plan.

Once the above are in place, he works with his team to achieve deadlines, or renegotiate dates in advance when necessary.

The failing leader who is changing and becoming objective oriented needs to also develop habits that will help him make his new found approach continuous. He needs to set challenging goals that will stretch him and his team; goals that align with the objective of the organization.

> "Failure comes only when we forget our ideals and objectives and principles."
>
> **Jawaharlal Nehru**

39

THE TRAP
OF QUICK
SUCCESS

I t is the aspiration of every leader to have a big break and rise to the highest height of their work.

This is very good however a leader may be swept under the carpet of quick success if they do not realize the consequences of such accelerated growth. This is because with quick and astronomical growth comes extra finance, opportunities, access, etc. when this happens many leaders have found themselves trapped in giving themselves to extravagance, instability and irresponsibility.

The likely trap of quick success is the intoxication it brings. A person who wants to avoid the failure of leadership through this challenge must ask himself:

□ What is the highest height I want to go to in my career?

- Who do I want to be when I reach that level?

- What do I consider to be no success?

- How will I know when I have enough?

- What are the specific measuring lines for success?

- How much of my personal identity is determined by the benchmarks of success which I have set?

> "Success comes before work only in the dictionary."
>
> **Anonymous**

#40

BEING SURROUNDED WITH POOR ADVISORS

In the Good book, the wisest man who ever lived, Solomon, was said to have his wisdom endowed upon him by God. However, at his passage the elders around him asked his son how he intends to rule them. The young man asked for permission to seek advice before he gave them an answer. Unfortunately, he turned to the wrong people and his response was.

> "The king's answer was harsh and rude. He spurned the counsel of the elders and went with the advice of the younger set, "If you think life under my father was hard, you haven't seen the half of it. My father thrashed you with whips; I'll beat you bloody with chains!""

1 Kings 12:13-14 (The Holy Bible, MSG)

With such a response from the young king, he was a failure from day one.

Many leaders have failed possibly because having expressed themselves through a special gift, talent or unusual prominence, they have ended up being surrounded by people who feed their ego and flatter them beyond imagination.

Many have failed because they chose to accept the counsel of men who were greedy for power but uninterested in the welfare of the organization that the leader stands at the helm of.

It was Albert Einstein who said: *"an empty stomach is not a good political advisor"*. A leader who for example surrounds himself with hungry people will only get the advice or counsel that will in turn make this people's pockets and stomachs filled.

Consultation is a major step and a good one before reaching some kind of decision in major and minor matters today; but if we have the wrong advisors the case of the young man (Rehoboam) earlier referred to, could be repeated either on a smaller scale or in a bigger way. He lost the kingdom and his own dynasty.

It is important to qualify who has your ears if leadership is not to result in failure. This is because in the multitude of counselling and that which is a good counselling there is always safety. Not every counsel will help a leader from failing.

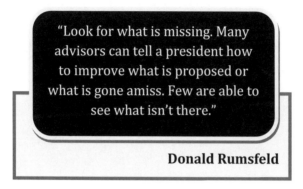

"Look for what is missing. Many advisors can tell a president how to improve what is proposed or what is gone amiss. Few are able to see what isn't there."

Donald Rumsfeld

#41 THOSE WHO BETRAY THEIR CONSCIENCE WHEN THE PRICE IS HIGH ENOUGH

The 1st November 2011 Management Today magazine quotes Oliver Bennett as saying: *"A trillion dollars a year are paid globally in bribes, it is a curse and will take more than the bribery act here and tougher laws in the US to sort out".*

Consider the case of Will Mitting, a man who set up a financial magazine in Malawi three years ago and found that he had to make bribes to printers and even payments to get invoices paid. There it is called a tip; if you don't pay it you'll be out of the game and you might not get your money. Global corruption has hit the corporate world.

The *UK Bribery Act* in force since July 2011 has already resulted in certain convictions, so too has the *US Foreign Corrupt Practice Act*. These two laws go as far as making it a crime punishable at home if any of its citizens were to give or take a bribe abroad.

Recently in the UK, the serious fraud office charged 71 year old Bill Lowther, alleging that he had conspired to pay the school fees of the son of the governor of a Vietnamese state owned bank; he had conspired to pay the school fee at Durham University.

> "There is no witness so dreadful, no accuser so terrible as the conscience that dwells in the heart of every man."
>
> **Anonymous**

The challenge of the betrayal of conscience is almost everywhere; a common routine in Russia and in most of Africa is for 'officials' to pop up after you have negotiated a contract and demand a procurement fee. What do you do when you are made to betray your conscience because the amount to make is so high?

The story is told of the man who was approached by a lobbyist who had boasted that anyone could be bought if their price were met. The man was offered $40,000 and he turned it down, then $50,000, $60,000 and finally the offer was raised to $80,000. At this point the principled man asked that the lobbyist be escorted off the premises. In his words he said: *"now be gone, you are getting too near my price",* still buttressing the fact that there is a point when the conscience may not be the most powerful policeman to stop a man from failing because of the betrayal of his conscience.

42

USING PEOPLE FOR PERSONAL ADVANCEMENT

As strange as this may sound it is a common practice on a day by day basis for certain leaders to use their subordinates and even where they are for personal advancement; instead of seeking the welfare of those who serve them.

There are many brilliant leaders who attain a high position; they have a track record of great achievements and success. The only challenge is that after a careful analysis of how they got to where, one may find that they have been using people for their own advancement.

To use people is a grave fault; the leaders who do this look upon others as being inferior to them while they consider their own interest of greater value and the people they use as inconsequential. They go about the act of using people by dominating, humiliating, isolating, intimidating and when that does not work; they apply threats, denial of opportunities or benefits and worse off they pick and choose who they want to promote or help, so the neglected can feel the impact of being set aside. A leader will fail if this is his approach.

> "What most people need to learn in life is how to love people and use things instead of using people and loving things"
>
> **Anonymous**

For leadership to be truly successful there is a need to recognize the fact that without the assistance of other people greatness may not be truly achieved. No man stands alone; we all stand on the shoulders of other people. The least a leader can show is gratitude for those who have been vision helpers.

Truly a man might have attained to the highest position and feel like a success but indeed part of his punishment is the fact that he is allowed to prosper in his delusion. So when we look for only our own thing and not the interest of other people we have failed in leadership.

> "Let each of you look out not only for his own interests, but also for the interests of others."
>
> **Philippians 2:4 (The Holy Bible NKJV)**

#43

FAILING TO BE AUTHENTIC

An authentic leader is the person who has chosen to live a life of integrity, honesty and forthrightness. Not only are they honest with everyone, they are also true to themselves; they do not deny their humanity neither do they deny their mistakes. They take responsibility for their ways so that they make room for learning and growing. Conversely when a leader goes in the opposite direction of this, our description of his leadership style and person becomes inauthentic and destined to fail.

An authentic leader keeps growing; he adjusts to the conditions that face him on a day by day basis. It is easier for an authentic leader to be honest with the people they come into contact with. This in turn helps them to develop a higher level of trust and goodwill between them and the followership.

In his book Authentic Leadership: courage in action, Bob Terry defines authentic leadership as: *"authenticity is knowing and acting on what is true and real inside yourself, your team and your organization and knowing and acting on what is true and real in the world"*. *"It is not enough to walk one's talk if one is headed off, or leading one's organization, community or nation off a cliff"*.

> **"Don't pretend to be someone you are not. It is better to suffer being who you are than it is to suffer trying to be someone that you are not."**
>
> **Unknown**

So inauthentic leaders make promises they cannot keep, they have hidden agendas and pretend when they are insincere in their motive. When leadership is not authentic it is prone to failure.

#44

A BROKEN FOCUS

When the focus of a leader is broken, danger is inevitable. A broken focus is the beginning of accidents.

Several years ago, I was driving on the motorway. I had an engagement to speak in a city in Africa. It was a long journey, four hours to be precise. Along the way I became hungry and stopped to buy some takeaway food. While driving I was focused on the food that I had placed on the front passenger seat and was eating because of the hunger pangs. In one split moment of focusing on the food and also driving at high speed, I drove off the road and into a ravine; by the time I lifted up my head, instead of seeing the motorway, all I saw was bush ahead. It took some time to get my bearings and realize that one simple act of broken focus had resulted in driving off the road.

Leadership is similar, when our focus is shifted from the important things; leaders simply lose sight of what is necessary and should be done. Remember, by leadership we are talking about people who have distinguished themselves in the past and have had a track record of achievement. They did not get there without thinking big and focusing well but with time as their focus shifts and their thinking becomes less, they begin to make mistakes and shift their focus from what should be the main thing. The laser like focus which brought them to where they are and raised them to the highest level becomes reduced by the trappings of leadership.

This include the danger of micro managing so that they focus on looking nice, being caught in minute details, the apparent presence of wealth and popularity, they become involved in minor decisions that could have been left to others.

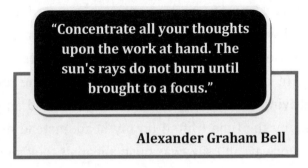

"Concentrate all your thoughts upon the work at hand. The sun's rays do not burn until brought to a focus."

Alexander Graham Bell

The kind of decisions which a leader should have on a list of *"don't dos"*; a continuous quest for perfection until the followership is driven off the cliff; the dangerous commitment that leads to the thought that busy means better; the trappings and the obsession with doing rather than becoming, should all be included.

When a leaders focus is broken he can become a failure. Yes, it is truly important for the leader to be willing, to roll up his sleeves and serve in any capacity where his ability may be needed but his focus can be broken if he is available to do almost everything. To keep your focus it is important to strive, to think on a higher level to make the transition from being a mere doer to a developer of people.

True leadership is not about just the things you can do but the people you can raise and how you can improve the people who follow you. When focus is broken, leadership has failed.

#45

POOR COMMUNICATION

The art of communication is the encoding and presentation of a message for it to be decoded by the receiver. It stands on the tripod of a message, the sender and the receiver.

It is a cardinal point and a necessity for quality leadership; followers cannot possibly understand a leader's intention if it has not been properly communicated. Communication will fail and the leadership will also if it is presented within an inappropriate context, without an understanding of the audience, if the thinking behind the communication is muddled and if those to whom the leader is speaking consider him to be the wrong spokesperson.

It is possible for the leader himself not to be clear as to the purpose and vision he carries. This lack of clarity is often times cloaked with confusion and ambiguity in the way it presents information. Many times despite the fact that a leader has not properly communicated, many have deluded themselves into believing that somehow almost through some clairvoyant gift the followers know their wishes and will carry them out. In fact, the opposite is true. Misunderstanding arises and the blame game begins.

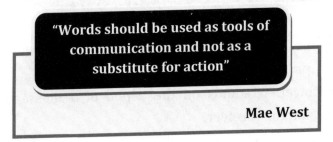

"Words should be used as tools of communication and not as a substitute for action"

Mae West

The followership as receivers of the message may be unclear as to the purpose of the message presented to them; it may sound illogical or lacking in structure. In the extreme, the receivers may even consider that the message presented is offensive in its tone and non-connecting. Many organizations have experienced failure because a leader has not studied the cultural perceptions of the people who they lead and use that as method for reaching the mind of the followership.

Communication from the leader can also fail if the timing is poor or the style used is ineffective for the particular setting. Communication also fails when the followership questions the ethics behind the message presented. To avoid failure a leader will need to qualify the style of his communication and to whom he is communicating. He may have to break his audience into various levels; the core group, the managerial and the corporate body. What is encoded for each of this group is dependent on what they need to know and do.

Communication may also be on the basis of who the leader is communicating with. For example: with the core group, what might be effective for the leader may be strategic writing or speaking; for the managerial, appealing to their emotional intelligence, coaching, mentoring, creating teams as well as listening. However for the corporate body which may include all stakeholders, there may be a need for employee relationship, image reputation management. If these approaches are overlooked leadership will fail.

#46

RISK AVERSION

In general leaders appear to be risk seeking, risk taking people. They are not blind thrill seekers; however leaders take risks and see the route which others avoid as a potential opportunity for making something new happen.

In some ways risk taking distinguishes leaders from managers. There are other differences between leaders and managers:

- Leaders are transformational; managers are transactional.

- Leaders sell; managers tell.

- Leaders are pro-active; managers are reactive.

- Leaders shape; managers enact.

- ☐ Leaders have passion, leaders have control, leaders have heart; managers have head.

- ☐ Leaders have personal charisma; managers have formal authority.

- ☐ Leaders set directions; managers plan the detail.

- ☐ Leaders know what is right; managers follow being right.

- ☐ Leaders give; managers take. Leaders seek; managers establish.

- ☐ Leaders take the blame; managers pass the blame.

However, a leader can find himself on the verge of breakdown because of things not being as progressive as they used to be; he finds himself entertaining the fear of failure rather than the desire to succeed and dwells more on past victories instead of creating new breakthroughs.

They are so afraid of whether they will be able to sustain performances to the level of past achievements.

Many leaders are often looking for what is an encore, trying to repeat the *good old days* and the longer a leader is successful, the higher their perception of the cost of failure. Therefore they dig their heels in and take no more risks.

When a leader is driven by fear of failure, he is unable to take the kind of risk that could break new grounds. Leadership is not recklessness, however when a leader is paralyzed by fear, he makes no move and gains no new ground.

> "The person who risks nothing, does nothing, has nothing, is nothing, and becomes nothing. He may avoid suffering and sorrow, but he simply cannot learn and feel and change and grow and love and live."
>
> **Leo F. Buscaglia**

A Chinese proverb says *"he who is afraid to throw the dice will never throw six"*. When leadership becomes risk averse, leadership fails.

#47

POOR SELF-MANAGEMENT

Success in leadership brings its own benefits. It gives the leader a level of attention, opportunities, platforms, and open doors; in a lot of cases success in leadership also brings financial benefits, public notoriety, connections and opportunities.

However it goes without saying that one of the things that may be difficult to manage once one becomes successful in leadership is yourself. If you think this is untrue, consider the fact that many are at the very height of their success and also throwing caution to the wind. We are surrounded by the consequences of decisions of executives who were involved in highly questionable ethics in Enron and WorldCom. We remember the doping charges brought against Marion Jones, the Gold medallist; we are perpetually confronted with agonizing accusations of child sex abuse that were brought against certain priests in the Roman Catholic Church. Need I mention the imprisonment of the onetime Mayor of Detroit, Kwame Kilpatrick. It seems to me that many people should have taken a vow that once they reach a level as high as the aforementioned individuals, they will do everything to protect the opportunities they have.

The challenge of poor self management in leadership is the fact that in a lot of cases many leaders are in the state or condition where they have to take care of themselves because no one else will.

If you do not have perceptive followers no one will sense the fatigue or tiredness you are going through. Leaders are also humans; they can be burnt out physically, emotionally, spiritually and psychologically. Leaders are not superheroes who are running on limitless emotional gas. Therefore if the emptiness and tiredness of a leader is not quickly noticed, heeded and handled, both he and the organization he leads may be heading towards a major disaster.

Self management or the preservation of a leader is not selfish but vital to the health of this person at the head of the organization. Leadership will fail if there is no self management procedure which the leader takes himself through.

How will a leader manage himself?

a. Take the initiative, be the first to volunteer to do certain things in your organization. Be willing to pay a price and serve others.

b. Practice discretion, learn to live by example and know when to say NO.

c. Set goals for your life; physical, emotional, spiritual, mental and financial. Clearly define to yourself what the meaning of life is.

d. Come up with new ideas everyday and use it to stretch your mind, your thoughts and your reach.

e. Be humble and give credit to other people; do not let the size of your ego be equal to the size of the office you occupy; or else if you get out of the office you might crash totally.

f. Believe in the people around you, see the quality in them and then go out and find that quality. This will help you even in your spare time to look for the homeless, the helpless, the poor, the widow and reach out to them. In the process you will feel refreshed and actualized.

g. Reject any form of pessimism; in fact have zero tolerance for negativity and doubts. That way as you keep your optimism high, you are able to achieve even more.

h. Never move away from the *why* and the *why not* questions of life. Always have a reason to wonder why. *Why do things happen? Why are things the way they are?*. Be curious, insatiably curious, question everything.

i. Be a champion of change to the environment, to your neighbourhood, to your country. Don't be a person who is known for apathy, complacency and boredom. Get excited, be part of the process in turning things around.

j. Care – compassion, sympathy and empathy should clothe your heart so that you reach out and notice the humanity around you. When you are so busy loving life, loving people and refreshing yourself; leadership will no longer be a burden to you but a blessing.

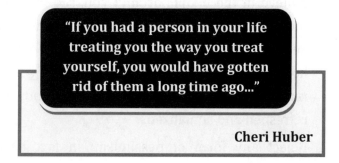

"If you had a person in your life treating you the way you treat yourself, you would have gotten rid of them a long time ago..."

Cheri Huber

48

A LACK OF PERSONAL GROWTH

The demands of leadership and the challenges which the 21st century leader is accosted with, makes it obvious that there is a need for a perpetual personal growth.

A leader needs to check different aspects of his personal approach to his work and see the area which requires development. If for example, the leader is impatient, this can become a broken cog in the wheel of success for the Leader.

In effect, leaders need a diverse range of approaches to growth. Some need to be street smart along with academic training. The reason for this is because today's leadership comes into contact with a diverse range of people, places and things.

A leader who does nothing to facilitate his own personal development will not change automatically. You will be the same person five years from now unless you are exposed to different sources of personal development. For example, books, seminars, associates, mentors etc.

The man who wants to fly with wings like eagles must not hang around turkeys. Leaders must learn how to hang out with other leaders who are doing well, who are achieving.

Personal growth prevents obsolescence; it renews your vision. It keeps you abreast of facts and gives you a continuous platform for success.

Growth for a leader may not come easily. He may have to look for people who are doing better or breaking new grounds. Ask for the opportunity to hang out with them, for them to be mentors, teach you, partner with you; whatever it takes to grow personally. Leadership fails when it stops growing.

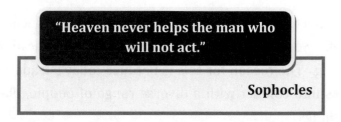

"Heaven never helps the man who will not act."

Sophocles

#49

A BREACH OF TRUST

Regardless of a country, culture or people; in spite of the organisation, church or nation, a major requirement for Leadership efficiency is trust. Trust in the Leader, trust in what they say, trust in their ability to deliver what they promise.

If Leadership is about setting an example that others should seek to emulate, one major area where that becomes necessary is that the trust of the people must not be breached. When trust is breached, the credibility of the leader has been seriously damaged.

This is the challenge when revelations begin to flood in about misconduct of leadership, either at corporate level or in small organisations.

When evidences begins to accumulate and suggest that the person or persons who have been called a leader or leaders have actually operated by a two faced approach to life, the eruption of the scandal will create a major destruction or shift in the level of trust. Particularly, if there has not been a disclosure or accountability by the leader.

> "A true friend never breaches the trust of his companion or stabs in his back. He is trustworthy and reliable. One should therefore always try to be a true and reliable friend. "
>
> **Sam Veda**

A most crucial shortage threatening our world today is not money, precious stones, oil or any other physical resource, it is the lack of quality leadership; people who know how to build trust and who show us their transparency. Rather, when people have not walked in a trustworthy manner, they try to hire those who to help to build their image.

Leaders are also humans. In order to build trust and not breach it, it may be wise to:

a. Treat employees, associates and those who are close to the Leader as adults, who are respected enough to be told the truth whether it is bad news or good news; rather than children who cannot be trusted to manage information or who could become traumatised.

b. Allow time for people to assimilate and deal with the upheaval that may come as a result of such disclosure.

c. It may be wise to cross-train people who will be leaving, with those who will inherit their work so that there is always transparency.

On a personal level a leader would need to:

a. Acknowledge that trust has been broken and not bury their head in the sand like Ostrich.

b. Admit the role that caused the breach of trust. In other words, the leader needs to muster the courage to humble himself and own up to his actions and how his action has affected the organisation.

c. Then apologise, asking for forgiveness and take steps to make amends to whoever may have been offended. Also explaining the reasons why the situation occurred may be helpful for people to truly understand what the leader may have gone through.

d. Then assess where the breach of trust may have

taken place. The breach of trust is sometimes shown in the leader not being:

A – Able   **B** – Believable   **C** – Connected or

D – Dependable

e. Amend and improve: Do all you can to rebuild trust. Find mentors and those who would create a structure around you to move on from failure to success.

#50

INTERPERSONAL INCOMPETENCE

Organisations are in the habit of promoting their best Engineers, Managers, Sales persons, Machine Operators, Accountants, Technicians, etc. Once these people have demonstrated a great skill in their chosen field, it leads to the assumption that they can also be good leaders. However, leadership competence is different from the skill they may have demonstrated in their chosen field.

Many are very good in the things they've trained in, or in the gifts they have, but they do not have any leadership training and even where that is provided following the promotion, it still does not guarantee a personal competence in relating to people.

Once these people have been promoted, then it becomes obvious that they are unable to motivate or carry others along. A key element which is the reason for their failure is that their interpersonal skills are failing.

> "The people with whom you work reflect your own attitude. If you are suspicious, unfriendly and condescending, you will find theses unlovely traits echoed all about you. But if you are on your best behavior, you will bring out the best in the persons with whom you are going to spend most of your working hours."
>
> **Beatrice Vincent**

Interpersonal competence starts with a self awareness; of your personal skills and behaviour and adjusting accordingly to be able to understand others.

Interpersonal competence is further strengthened by building strong lasting mutual and beneficial relationships with other people. It is further enhanced by the developing the ability to resolve conflict in a positive manner. A leader who is detached and unemotional, who does not know how to build bridges with others, cannot be said to be a strong leader and is likely to fail.

To avoid failure, Leadership would require:

a. An understanding of one's self and others too.

b. A building of relationships

c. Developing conflict resolution skills

d. Learning to maintain self-disclosure as a way of allowing people to see the humanity of the leader.

e. Providing emotional support for people so that they know that the leader is truly not there to bark out orders but understands their need and is building bridges towards them.

51

WHEN LEADERSHIP SETS THE WRONG EXAMPLE

At the time of the writing of this book, an Italian luxury cruise liner entered shallow waters, hit the rocks and was shipwrecked.

Many passengers died, the majority were rescued. The failure of leadership in this situation was that firstly, the Captain, who had given conflicting reasons for what had happened, was found to have been amongst the first to jump ship to safety. In such circumstances the Captain should have stayed in his boat to supervise the rescue of passengers. He was said to have claimed that he accidentally fell into the rescue boat.

It is an absolute truth that how a leader behaves whether as a parent, organisational head, spiritual or secular will influence the behaviour of other people.

Good examples help us to go further, see further and achieve more. In the words of **Isaac Newton:** *"If I have* *seen further than others it is because I was standing on the shoulders of giants."*

Leadership sets the wrong example when it does not walk its talk. It sets the wrong example when it feels that some things are ok for the leader to do because they are above the employee's or followers.

It is not often difficult to know a bad example in leadership.

Firstly, they use threats and punishment to motivate followers.

Secondly, they use fear tactics to get results. They tell people that if production doesn't pick up around here, somebody will lose their job; 'heads will roll'.

Thirdly, they practice self servicing power. When a leader uses power in an inappropriate way, it becomes intoxicating and on the other hand it produces the wrong result.

Fourthly, leaders who are bad examples create factions, in-groups and out groups. They seem to enjoy an *'us versus them'* atmosphere.

> "If you must hold yourself up to your children as an object lesson, hold yourself up as a warning and not as an example."
>
> **George Bernard Shaw**

52

POOR DECISION MAKING

G enerally, all leaders set out to make good decisions. However, the results which follow have often shown that good leaders can make bad decisions. The challenge starts with the fact that we all place leaders on a pedestal and assume that leaders automatically make good decisions for the followers or damn the followers.

On the contrary, many times leaders make bad decisions and even frequently make worse decisions than their followers. Leaders are not always the best people to make the decision for organisations; for a group of people or for any business.

We are surrounded with the evidences of bad decisions from good Leaders. An example is the decision of Jurgen Schrempp, the CEO of Daimler Benz, who decided - against internal opposition - to acquire Chrysler of America and nine years later had to let go through some kind of agreement because of the apparent likelihood of bankruptcy.

Another example is the decision by politicians or presidents of nations to annul certain elections, simply because it doesn't favour them or to confer and have *town house* discussions with only the privileged few on national matters before making decisions that affect the majority of the population.

Decisions to dig heels in even in a changing climate on certain matters, show poor decision making come for various reasons:

a. A lot of decisions from some of such leaders are purely reactive and possibly an answer to an issue that has been raised by others

b. Bad decisions come from self interest when the leader elevates the benefit of the decision for themselves and their cohorts above the population.

c. There are pre-judgments as to what the result would be if they make the decision without looking at the various consequences of the decisions being made.

d. Attachments: Often times leaders make decisions because of an attachment to the subject of discussion. Sometimes leaders have been known to keep members of their executive board because of a certain kind of attachment - even if the persons are seemingly not performing.

e. Political Reasons; This is diverse and dependent on the political terrain. Some nations elevate and give positions not on the basis of competence but geographical connection of the persons involved.

Political pressure could also include giving jobs to 'the boys' because they are part of the ruling party - even if they do not have the skill or competence.

Often times these decisions are made to the detriment of the nation and with a blatant action of overlooking competent and skilled people who could have done better in the particular area.

Having said this, it must also be admitted that sometimes intelligent and good decisions may be flawed from the onset and may result in a loss or a damaging consequence on the organisation.

A possible approach to preventing poor decision making and leadership failure may be:

a. To engage in real debate. Thus allowing many people to contribute to the discussion.

b. To consider alternatives and allow oneself to be put in a box early on the matter being discussed.

c. To learn from past mistakes.

d. Zero in on what is important without allowing the emotions to take over.

#53

INSECURITY

W hat is insecurity?~It is the feeling of not being good enough to meet the challenges of a situation or to face the issues of life.

Insecurity gives a sense of helplessness in the face of problems, conflicts or concern. It makes one feel like they do not fit in or are out of sync with those who are their peer groups. It is the fear of being discovered to be inadequate, ill fitted, unsuited to meet the responsibilities at home, school and, as it applies to our subject, leadership.

An insecure leader is even more dangerous because when one feels that he is inadequate to handle a matter or incompetent to handle life's challenges, woe betide that leader if in his group a person rises who has a degree of confidence and a focus that makes them able.

Poor self esteem based on family experiences is shockingly high within the realms of leadership. It has made many leaders to have the sense of always climbing but never reaching the top. In some cases, where a leader is an achiever, he feels inadequate and his success seems like a failure to him. They are always looking for validation in the wrong places. There is a sense of lacking in support or reinforcement where they live, work, play or those whom they serve.

Insecurity often times is a by-product of early rejection, disapproval of being unaccepted. It creates an inner turmoil which results in a lack of direction or a bewilderment as to where to go. Whenever insecurity is present in a person, they could achieve but they will either be perpetual state of comparing themselves with someone else, or in some cases it may result in victimizing the followership if that is what makes the leader feel strong on the outside.

Many dictators and leaders who have gone wrong have been known to have backgrounds of rejection and inadequacies that were never dealt with.

One of the worst tendencies which set a leader up for failure is insecurity. As a matter of fact, there is more damage done by it particularly to young and upcoming leaders than anyone else.

It makes such people vulnerable by reason of the position they have attained because it allows them to be consumed by pride.

> "Insecurities have the ability to shape and mold our minds to live with everything that's bad; like crying on the inside, while smiling on the outside...thus creating pain...but, alas, I have the answer; forget about what you thought and enjoy (embrace) what you feel"
>
> **Jeremy Aldana**

Dictionary.com defines Insecurity as the *lack of confidence or assurance, self doubt, the quality or state of being insecure or instability.*

Insecurity is a double headed hydra which makes people take on pride to cover-up or a false humility because of an inability to stand tall and occupy a position.

The other words which convey the same meaning would be changeability, fickleness, fluctuation, inconsistency, wavering, weakness and unpredictability.

We are not only exposed or vulnerable to each of these things when we are young but rather it becomes even more manifest when we are in situations which stretch us, when demands are made upon us that seem to be above our ability to handle or cope with.

The success orientated society of the 21st Century also doesn't seem to help because when a man fails, he is seen as not being seen good enough. In leadership, some leaders do not immediately realise that the actions they exhibit suggest insecurity.

Firstly, when they try to exercise too much control and have to be in charge of everything, or when they refuse to take advice from anyone and seem to be the only wise one among the people they serve. Insecure leaders also like to raise a standard so high and operate by a legalistic approach, making them control freaks. Several other characteristics that may have been mentioned in other parts of this book could reflect insecurity:

This includes micro-managing, refusing to delegate, constantly yelling at staff, creating teams of 'yes men' and not those who challenge the decision of the leader, backstabbing or creating the atmosphere for it, being the controller of knowledge and therefore making everyone come to the leader, delaying decisions and flip flopping afterwards, name dropping to show how important the leader is and who they know, defending when they should explore and being vulnerable when it could help them or even correct.

Insecure Leaders take things personally. When a criticism comes forward, they do not see it as a criticism of a decision, action or opinion; they see it as a criticism of their person. In some circumstances, an insecure leader is unable to say **NO** without feeling guilty.

They are experts at trading blame. They prefer to share the blame with other people and then take all the credit. In some circumstances, they blame higher authority for all the tougher decisions that went wrong. Insecure leaders have a difficulty trusting people because they do not trust themselves.

However, they do not use that exact word to describe the state of their own condition. They won't delegate because of the fear of failure and mistakes. And in the end they drop the ball and make more mistakes.

It is very difficult to describe insecure leaders and insecurity in general and not find a little of it rubbing on us because essentially we are all fallen humanity. The ways out would include a desire and an attempt to believe that we all have a purpose and a place and we belong in this world.

This should be followed by the importance of people knowing that you are human and leadership does not exclude you from that.

A good leader who wants to overcome his insecurities would need to read the biographies of others and see the weakness and strength of leaders; what they did when their decisions went wrong, then let opportunity motivate them rather than fear.

Decisions that are based on fear do not always end up being profitable. When an insecure person is confronted with a decision that seems tough, they need to make it known. So they do not make it look like it is a walk through the park and when the consequences come, they bury their head in the sand.

To overcome insecurity the discussion, debate or matter being confronted should be centred on the issues and not people. Small people discuss people, great minds discuss issues. In the process, give others what you wish they would give you. If you wish they give you attention, give the same out. Act and speak with gentle confidence not over-confidence. Over-confidence in itself may be a sign of insecurity.

Leadership must realise that making decisions should be the primary thing and not the pursuit of success for its own sake. As one's confidence grows, he needs to act with optimism, even if the result will not be as positive as expected.

If you must compare yourself, let it be with yourself and not with others. All men have their giftings and abilities, and beyond yourself learn to pray.

And finally, the path to overcoming is trodden upon by taking trusted people into our confidence and letting them know our insecurities.

#54

NO SUCCESSION PLAN

N o one seems to want to leave their position of leadership. From Presidents who seek a change of constitution in order to perpetuate their term; to founders of organisations who believe it is their right to found it and stay there until their death. There are also suppressive CEOs, Heads of organisations, who consider it a thing of celebration that no one could do the job like they do.

A Succession Plan – What is it?

It is actually planning for the future and preparing the organisation in readiness for somebody else to progress it further from where the leader stops. Actually, success without a Successor is failure.

A Succession Plan is learning to focus on the future of the organisation, knowing full well that you might not be there at a time when that future arrives.

Why is a succession plan necessary?

a. For the sake of continuity. The organisation which dies with the current leader has failed; not because it does not have the potential to expand but because the leader has failed to realise that true leadership is raising the future generation. A good leader should be able to ask himself *'who will replace me someday'* and such a thought should excite him to pave way for them to begin to come up.

b. A succession plan also is necessary because it gives room for creativity. Generations change and people have different perspectives. One generation is fading away, another is rising. The generation that was born almost 40 years ago is different to the ones who were born after the 2nd World War.

☐ The new generation long for a sense of belonging.

☐ They value authenticity, transparency and humility.

☐ They desire a change in the world, environmentally and geographically.

☐ They find meaning in things that are mysterious, metaphoric, paradoxical and artistic.

This generation is the *'Facebook'* generation, the *'MySpace'* generation, the generation who has had an opportunity to rub minds with the computer; the micros and the mobile phone. They prefer the practical and the immediate to the dogmatic and bureaucratic. They bring creativity that is fluid and continuous.

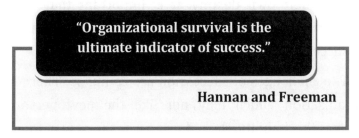

"Organizational survival is the ultimate indicator of success."

Hannan and Freeman

c. A succession plan is also necessary because it helps an organisation, nation, people, places to experience capacity building. Today's success may be great for now but the capacity of the future would obviously be much better. At the wake of the 80s, new information and discoveries was every ten years. In the 90s, it was every year. In 2000 and beyond, it was every month. Nowadays, there is a fresh and new breakthrough in almost every remit, every day.

A leader who therefore fails to prepare his organisation, nation, and people for succession will find that it won't be long before they're caught up with obsolescence.

d. The next reason which makes a Succession Plan a necessity is the creation of the future. However, succession plans often are more saddled with challenges than possibilities. Oftentimes because of the current leadership which tends to resist it. Leaders often never like to let go. However, like our children who must at one time move away from us and sail away into their own destiny, it is important that a leader realises that a succession plan is rather part of his success.

The challenges of succession are complex. There is the organisation which may not like the new person but prefers the stability, the old brings; or the new person who may not like the new organisation because he observes there are things that require change.

Succession is sometimes difficult because the family of the new Leader is having challenges adjusting to the current place; corporate culture is not friendly but rather adversarial. The new leader may fail because he is unable to win a following since his style and interpersonal skills have not been developed; which also means that his values and belief system do not match with the organisation. Sometimes there is a failure of succession because the new leader truly is dynamic and the ability to make the organisation succeed but the old guard along with the old leader are sabotaging his efforts.

And yet all these may not be as difficult as the old leader who fails to totally disappear over the horizon but keeps making excuses and has reasons for perpetually being around the organisation and making it look as if someone is trying to abort his baby.

The only thing which makes succession very difficult, is the departing leader. Why? Well, they may have a fear of retirement, a resistance to change, there is also a possibility of him not making adequate financial preparation for the future. Several people have moved on and allowed a successor only to find that they did not have enough to keep them busy and engaged in a profitable way.

e. A succession plan is not a walk through the park. There may also be challenges particularly if the leader who is departing seems to draw his sense of worth and confidence from the position and title. This possibly accounts for the reason why many Third World Presidents and Heads of States have difficulty in transition into regular civilian life and handing over to someone else.

On the contrary, they perpetuate their position and make it look as if no one is adequate in a nation of teeming millions; no one is able to replace them; which in itself is a sure sign of failure.

When leadership fails to prepare and produce a Succession Plan, it could not be described as a success. Within that context the leader has failed.

Correcting this situation may be by developing a mentoring system from day one. No one ever arrives fully ready to take on a major responsibility. The onus rests on a true leader to see potential in people, develop the ability to tolerate mistakes and abrasiveness and challenge such potential people to become the best that they can be. In raising future leaders, of course, the leader is risking his own reputation because he may have made the mistake of choosing the wrong protégé.

However, it is better to impart Leadership skills in other people than to do nothing at all and feel that in this way the organisation will always need him.

Leadership is truly a major investment. Those who are at the higher echelon in any organisation invest emotionally, psychologically, musically and otherwise. Sometimes the dividends may have not been fully grown, when it may be time to depart.

However, a leader may look at it in a different way and realise that he has made a contribution in his lifetime and truly prepares the coming generation to succeed him, whether he is remembered or not.

#55

DERAILMENT

In August 2009 a tidal wave hit the banking industry of the country of Nigeria which led to the removal of five CEOs of banks. This action carried, out by the Apex Bank (the Central Bank of Nigeria) was as the consequence of the shocking result of the true health of Nigerian Banks. (Apex Bank when deployed resident examiners on a special examination of the nations' banks). One major issue for international investors was whether the extent of these banks that were exposed extended to the nineteen others.

The Apex Bank discovered among many other things a compromise of due process and the deliberate flaunting of corporate laws. CEOs of these banks were reported to have amassed untold wealth within a short time and in some cases owning properties which they turned around and rented back to the banks. It may not be unique to them; frequently an exceptional executive may encounter a corporate trap door, fall through and end up derailing because of the pressure which comes with the opportunity.

Many executives have stepped in to critical situations where their experience, training and being savvy has not been able to protect them and in the end they fail. In some circumstances, boards have taken over; that way it brings the exceptional executive job to an unceremonial end.

The 21st century seems to have brought along with the multiple success and opportunities a corporate trap door. Today we observe an intensifying global challenge, instability in the capital market and increasing demand for personal and corporate transparency.

All these make the need for the executive to be savvy and experienced or else fall victim to the treacherous physical, mental and political gauntlet that comes along with it.

In the 21st century, it is becoming observable that CEOs are no longer remaining in their offices for a longer period because of the challenge of derailment.

Derailment comes in several ways

a. Business Failure

One of the most obvious reasons for derailment is when business fails through the lack of liquidity, inability to access capital and credit, plunging market capitalisation or a failed financial performance.

A CEO who cannot get his organization to turn this around has failed the test of executive's survivability.

b. Another major reason for derailment is with the advent of the internet and sources of information like *'Wiki Leaks'*, personal or ethical compromise have been dusted up and put in public eye. Such unsettling information has made boards across the world make quick decisions and change their CEOs.Where the board is made up of *'Yes Men'*, regulators have been known to step in.

c. A more major reason for derailment may be the inability of the person who has been elevated to the position of CEO. Bad decisions, wrong actions, incubate and end up birthing situations that bring discredit and eventual decline to the organization. The failure of such executive becomes undeniable and irreversible

What are the signs of derailment? Why do leaders fail through derailment?

There are a few telltale signs which once they manifest; they are a red flag and may mean such a leader is setting himself up for failure.

a. Maladjustment

A derailing leader loses focus under pressure, is unable to develop a sense of self-awareness and then becomes sceptical, suspicious and obsessive as to what can go wrong in his organisation. This leads such a person to look for signs of betrayal among staff and misses the whole purpose of leadership which amongst many things is to develop others.

b. Over ambition

An over ambitious executive is in the path of derailment because over ambition makes other people feel invisible, overwhelmed others and intimidated. It also creates competitive rivalry.

An over ambitious leader disengages from others, problems and the organisation; he focuses more on what he can become, achieve or do and in the end he manipulates the system because he feels that the end justifies the means.

c. Lack of interpersonal sensitivity

Some of the things we deal with here have been dealt with in other parts of this book. However when a leader fails to develop interpersonal competence; he becomes reluctant to address personnel and performance problems. Rather, he is argumentative, abrupt, insensitive to the people around him, cannot be pleased, is too tough and is critical of other people. He fails to provide timely and sufficient feedback to those who work with him. A detached leader has derailed and has failed.

d. Over inquisitiveness

The strength of leadership is to be visionary, creative and anticipatory; to be curious and carry the staff along in balancing innovation with practicality but when the leader begins to lack initiative and the ability to be inquisitive and work on what could give ground breaking success in the future; such leader reverts to old standards, pragmatic solutions, narrow vision and sometimes totally withdraws and settles for average results.

e. Unteachable

Being a leader should not make one unteachable. This weakness in leadership is what becomes a reason for derailment.

When a leader fails to stay up to date with the area of his responsibility, whether in technical matters or facts about the job; an unteachable mind will make a leader neglect to invest in new skills and processes for improvement. He becomes forgetful, loses sight of the facts, he is rather aggressive to adopt the old ways of doing things and behaves as if he knows all things. While true leadership makes one open to new experiences, training and adaptability. When these red flags manifest, a leader may have derailed from the original purpose of the organisation.

Derailment is a by product of taking wrong steps in critical times or situations. Any organisation can go through a tough time, but the tough time should not end up being a trap door which ends up holding the leader and those who work with him in a perpetual merry go round without moving forward.

The antidote to derailment will be to create an inner circle; a group of people whom the leader or executive trusts, is open to and can receive advice and coaching from. It could be mentors from previous organizations or specialist consultants who can help him.

This inner circle which a leader has created and enlisted will help to protect his dreams and vision by sharing wisdom and providing insight. An inner circle is able to give warnings because they observe the early signs. An inner circle is emotionally detached from the situation and can therefore have valid and valuable judgement.

The inner circle helps such a leader to shape his thoughts and processes; they put his decisions to test and help him to observe the areas where he has failed to see.

Derailment can also be prevented by the leader as he becomes able to admit that he has **Achilles heel** – `to thyself be true'.* An increased awareness of our weaknesses helps us to adjust better, to employ people and make them our strength in the area of our weakness.

By the time one is of kindergarten age, certain patterns and manner of life have been shaped. They only increase no matter what training we take. Behavioural patterns do not go away easily; this hard wired persona of us may be easily observed by others who have chosen to look carefully. Such people are then able to help the leader know where the area of his strength is.

A socio-metric test may not exactly be the best way to observe and then overcome because sometimes the leader is involved in the test he can influence the result.

When leaders have been confronted with the challenge, two negative actions have sometimes been adopted, a *flight* or a *fight*. Both are counterproductive because running away from issues does not resolve anything, neither is choosing to fight it out because when it gets bloody there may be more damaging revelations at the end. A flight from a situation will give the impression that the leader is insecure, mistrustful, withdrawn and risk averse. Fighting may suggest that he intimidates and manipulates.

e. It is important for the leader to develop his ability to read the situation.

Derailment can be avoided if the leader can become wise enough to read the context. Having read the context he can now develop a method for handling issues.

A leader who takes on an organization should get to know the context, protocol and boundaries; he should find the keys that unlock the whole communication, collaboration and management system of a place instead of coming with an attitude that suggests that he has come with a *Gestapo* approach to change things by force.

Reading the situation is a skill that can be learnt; it is amazing to know that making friends of everyone from the man at the gate to the reception clerk could give one a clear perception of what is going on but along with this; the intuitive skills of the leader will protect him from derailment in such a situation.

f. Lastly, maybe a master protection from derailment will be a teachable spirit or a learning agenda.

This comes with the skills of listening, the acceptance of failure when it becomes apparent; the leader must realize that today's world does not seem to be fair; everything we do is in the full view of everybody, from employees to the stakeholders, bloggers to those who go on the internet and the media.

In a nutshell, the chances of derailment are very obvious but at the same time the chances of success are even bigger because the leader now has more information at his fingertips than previous executives have done.

CONCLUSION

In the past 25 years, organizational culture, systems and operations which were thought to be fail safe have been seen to collapse.

Major corporations have suffered from systems implosion. At the same time, nations like Iraq and Afghanistan have been invaded to bring about change, democracy and new leadership. Others have experienced a revolution and an implosion, particularly the Arab Spring. The wind which blew across the Middle East brought a change to Tunisia, Egypt, Yemen and Libya, is still blowing.

Where the wind has not blown, particularly in developing nations of the third world, there is an oxymoron, a contradiction. Many of these nations have natural, human and mineral resources and yet they are underdeveloped.

These various settings described seem to have one common challenge - Failed Leadership.

Why Do Leaders Fail?

There are several reasons given in this book. However, it includes the fact that leaders fail when their vision is unclear and they do not walk the talk, when they refuse to learn or develop those who walk with them.

The importance of this subject cannot be overemphasized because if we fix the leaders we will fix the world.

It is astonishing how little
what one actually sees has to
do with ones painting.
To start with Nature paints
with light, whereas we have to
make do with inadequate
pigments which are not even
approximations to what is
seen by the eye. Then there
is the question of 3 dimensions
& space, which we have to
imitate by subterfuge or
trickery. And then all the
detail seen & registered
inescapably by the eye,
impossible to transcribe.
It is not the

Venetian red or perhaps
burnt sienna - Cobalt for
skies, a slight use of yellow
ochre & terre-verte. Sometimes
he seems to use a dark blue
or even ultramarine mixed
with Indian red?? Occasionally
a bluish black - is it
Payne's grey? Or is it ultra
+ black mixed? The nude
from the Petit Palais seems
to consist entirely of black &
white mixed with burnt
sienna.
    I find the constant
use of terra verte for

The Eternal Moment

The Eternal Moment

Essays and a Short Story
by

Angelica Garnett

Puckerbrush Press
Orono, Maine

Acknowledgements:
Some of these essays have appeared in or for:
The Charleston Newsletter; *The Charleston Magazine*;
Anthony d'Offay; *Recollections of Virginia Woolf
by her contemporaries*, Ed. Joan Russell Noble;
The Bloomsbury Workshop.

Cover drawing and end papers from a sketchbook
by Angelica Garnett

First Printing May, 1998
Second Printing September, 1999

ISBN 0-913006-65-3

Printed in the United States of America
by Howland's Printing Company, Old Town, Maine
Bound by Furbush-Roberts, Bangor, Maine

Contents

The Eternal Moment

FOREWORD

The Passage of Time

Writing about the past is different from thinking about it since, although you can't write without thinking, you can of course do the opposite, and I am sometimes afraid of doing it too much. Faced with writing something, I have, of course to plunge into that deep well which seems to lie at the centre of one's being, an obscure lake in a nebulous country. One looks for reflections, and finds for the most part only those of oneself, narcissus-like, looking up with an expression hard to recognise, wavering in the depths, distorted by the passage of time.

Since I now see myself as having been exceptionally unaware of what I was like, and therefore equally oblivious of the efforts of other people to make contact with me, what is it I am trying to remember, and how far do any of these memories correspond to any kind of truth? How far am I to be trusted? Or is the concept of such a truth to be questioned?

I know my memory to be factually unreliable: it is subjective, obscured often by prejudice or egocentric emotion, longing to express a hyper-subtle sympathy that is impossible to put into words. These qualities are contradictory, so that I wonder what the value of the memory can be that is born of such mixed parentage? Facts are essential: of this there is no doubt. Their exist-

9

ence, or rather their recognition, can change the very nature of our feelings. If you later discover that someone was absent when you had taken their presence for granted, or vice versa, your entire understanding of the scene or event has to be re-examined, sieved and mixed again like the sauce from which you omitted the lemon juice, or in which you inadvertently left a lump or two, and it may be this sieving that is the most important part of the operation. It certainly has its bearing on the slow accumulation of those little bits of knowledge which enable one to think, towards the end of one's life, that one is beginning to know oneself.

But no one will ever know how complete this knowledge is, and although it is only to oneself that this matters, we will never know either. If indeed it does matter, it is certainly not in any final, one-off way. The images that come to mind are ones related to time, for example climbing a ladder or a mountain or, in euphoric moments, of rising like a hot air balloon into the unknown stratosphere. Or visions of clear water where the sediment has sunk to the bottom, or cellars which contain hidden riches. One needs time in which to climb, time to accumulate anything. But in the end, as with the caddis worm, it adds to one's volume, even perhaps to one's weight.

Why should one want to be heavy? Simply perhaps because one is not? Heaviness in fact seems undesirable, but moral weight estimable – at least to me, who never had any such thing. When I think of those among whom I grew up, I don't think any of them had it either. Vanessa had authority – often flawed by sudden doubt – and an emotional presence equalled by no one else. Moral weight and Duncan were like the North and South Pole – unimaginable together. Virginia was either all brilliance or melancholy, and Clive's authority, when exercised, was not moral. Neither I think was Roger Fry's. The only person who had a good deal of this quality, who seemed in fact bathed in it, was

Leonard, and although it was probably this that upset some people, like Duncan, it says a good deal for both him and Bloomsbury that they maintained intimate relations.

I see now how much I took the family for granted, how unthinkable it was and how shattering it would have been had any of them drifted away or – still more devastatingly – quarrelled to the point of no longer inviting us or coming to see us. When Virginia and Leonard came to tea, it was an intensification of our normal existence: we welcomed them with cries of joy, never for one moment questioning their equal pleasure in seeing us. This gave our lives an extraordinary rhythmic certainty, since they came to Charleston and we went to Rodmell more or less once a week. The same intimate contact was maintained during the London winters, often in Clive's Gordon Square flat where we met for dinner.

Clive's gift was for hospitality, and he played his role well, instinctively offering us our favourite dishes: peaches for Vanessa, trout for Virginia and still champagne for us all. When we left in the late evening, the air was full of the smoke of cigars, including Virginia's together with Vanessa's French cigarettes, a lingering if evanescent wreath in the stagnant air, testimony to an evening of enjoyment and a lifetime based on the art of communication.

Forcalquier, France, 1996

I

My Parents: Vanessa Bell and Duncan Grant

For myself, as one of its children, Bloomsbury seems to have two hearts, beating both in opposition to and in tune with each other. One is the literary heart, and the other is the quieter, less tumultuous heart of the painters. This is the one I was closest to but which, because it was less articulate, most people know less about. I have therefore chosen to talk about my parents, Vanessa Bell and Duncan Grant, both in their human and their artistic relationship, since the one is almost indistinguishable from the other.

If the Stephens were aristocrats of intellectual and literary London Duncan, though the son of a younger son, was the member of an ancient family with its roots in the land of Scotland. His cousin was a Laird and Duncan was frankly proud of his antecedents both on his mother's and his father's side. In the context of Bloomsbury however he was first and foremost a cousin of the Stracheys, as his father was Lady Strachey's brother. When he first appeared on the London scene it was in this light he was accepted since, in contradistinction to the Stephens and their friends, he was not a University man, and his parents, having spent most of their lives in the East, were virtually unknown.

At first sight however Duncan and the Stracheys were light years apart. Although Sir Richard Strachey had held an important administrative post under the British Raj, and many of his children had been to and worked in India, none of them had, I think, spent their childhood there. Their view of India was roughly speaking political whereas, having spent his infancy in the arms of an ayah, Duncan's was emotional and aesthetic in character. Neither had he been brought up by Lady Strachey, that passionate matriarch, to put the values of the intellect first and foremost. Though he was sent to school Duncan, by the most passive of all rebellions, rejected education and afterwards refused to take his normal place in society, reserving for himself the role of clown – a gentle but uncompromising attitude towards conventionality. According to my husband, David Garnett, the Stracheys tended to despise him for his lack of knowledge which, in their short-sighted eyes, implied or suggested lack of intelligence. In Bloomsbury's view this was the unforgiveable sin, and one of Duncan's triumphs was that while he never boasted either of his education or his intelligence he managed to live down this assumption, and forced Bloomsbury, in connection with him, to think again.

A Scotsman to the marrow of his bones with all the intuition of the Celt Duncan had, during his childhood spent in the East, also absorbed the classic detachment of the Oriental. It was an early impression made on a highly sensitive nature, and was to return more explicitly at the end of his life, giving him the other-worldly air of a Yogi. Though he was in a straight-forward sense a visionary, he was no romantic idealist, or at least not in daily life. He had plenty of Scottish wisdom and common-sense which implied an acceptance of his own and other people's limitations. His respect for other people's identities and the recognition that everyone was in his or her own way doing their best, was a passport to everyone's favour. He was no mere perfectionist, and was much better pleased to laugh over the fact that no one ever reaches the top of the tree, than condemn them for failure – a point of view which also owes something to the Oriental attitude.

He quickly became persona grata in Bloomsbury, where his affair with Lytton Strachey and Vanessa's brother Adrian, left no doubt about his homosexuality. Though unkempt and penniless Duncan was as beautiful as Adonis, a favourite image which later took up residence as a life-size plaster nude in the garden at Charleston. Though not without consciousness of the effect his looks produced on others, Duncan did not allow this to inhibit his relationships and was singularly free of personal vanity. This rare combination, together with his readiness to be amused and to take other people on trust, guaranteed his acceptance in a group of young people that was, on the whole, very much on the defensive.

After leaving Kensington for Bloomsbury Vanessa founded the Friday Club, making it possible for artists to see not only their work but each other, and it was here that she first saw Duncan, when she was 26 and he a mere 20. Their meeting reminds me of two boats that were later to meet in the China Sea passing each other in the night, without a sign of recognition. Vanessa was on the verge of discovering what life had to offer her, which at that moment by no means included Duncan. For him she was both inaccessible and irrelevant. She had by then exhibited very little of her work and he may well have wondered whether, as an artist, she was serious – so many young women were not, and she had plenty of other preoccupations.

Duncan himself was deeply serious: that is to say he was prepared to work extremely hard though, except in an idealistic way, he was not ambitious. No doubt he wanted to be as great a painter as it was in him to be, but he was not interested by riches or

15

renown and he did not care a rap for the impression he made on others. If he sometimes appeared ready to throw seriousness out of the window in favour of fun it was partly due to confidence in his gift, of which he could afford to spill a little here and there. He felt that, with such a thread to follow, he could never go far wrong.

Both Duncan and Vanessa had been brought up – though Vanessa more so – in the shadow of late Victorianism, and each had rejected, or thought they had, the values of their parents. In each case this was a compromise, but there was also a profound difference of attitude: while Vanessa swallowed her father's atheism and rationalism whole, she felt herself rejected and therefore rejected him – emotionally. Duncan however continued to love and respect his parents, while refusing to fall in with their innate conventionality. The reactions of each were characteristic. Vanessa was largely blinded by prejudice whereas Duncan, though passive, was completely clear about where his resistance ended and his affections began. He could afford to be a lover of tradition, both social and artistic, whereas Vanessa's sophisticated background imposed obligations that were both more lofty and more confused.

During the eight years that had elapsed between their first meeting and the beginning of their love-affair – roughly from 1905 to 1913 – a great deal had happened to Vanessa. Shortly after meeting Duncan at the Friday Club she married Clive Bell, and it was not irrelevant to ask: what, apart from having children, was her concept of marriage? It was not, like Virginia's, a passionate commitment to an intellectual companionship, which depended for its success on mutual honesty. It was something less clear-cut, less crystalline, less considered, since for Vanessa the question was complicated by the fact that she longed for sexual fulfilment.

She took her own honesty for granted, as indeed she took so

much else, and gave little thought to the more austere ethical or psychological questions. Even though, before marriage, she scolded Clive for his lack of seriousness, something in her tone of voice implied a maternal and certainly not an enquiring attitude. Her manner was not that of someone on equal terms, but more that of an elder sister reproving her brother for playing truant at school. Whereas Virginia and Leonard, when they eventually married, were a young couple preparing to struggle and work side by side, Vanessa and Clive conformed far more closely to the conventional concept of the cavalier and his lady, the one admiring and gallant, the other typical of what used to be known as "so feminine"; submissive and pliable on the one hand while determined to have her own way on the other.

Vanessa never really knew what equality meant. She had always been the eldest, she had always belonged to an élite and – more to the point – she felt she had never been truly loved. It was in spite of this that, prompted by the extraordinary generosity of her nature, she tried to compensate for this humiliating circumstance by accepting a degree of responsibility for others that ought never to have been asked of her. Too young to realise the dangers of such a situation, she evaded a too harsh reality by dreaming, and thus became insulated against other people's claims for recognition. Thus, though she was committed to looking after them materially, she took little notice of their spiritual needs which left her, if not unmoved, feeling inadequate. One of the minor but significant results of this state of things was that she was always either too arrogant or too humble; she was either coolly indifferent or she overidentified. Her sense of proportion, so cried up by Virginia, was in reality fragile and uncertain.

At first Clive was unaffected by these subtle complications, since he knew that he had conquered her sexually. He was too much of an egotist to bother about the subjective element, knowing only that the mysteries of Vanessa made her doubly attrac-

17

tive. Selfish as he was he thought he could do as he liked and was unfaithful to her with at least one other woman, from the very beginning of their marriage. I have talked elsewhere about Clive's flirtation with Virginia which took place so soon after that event, and will not repeat myself here. But it was another infidelity, albeit a-sexual. Within the first 18 months of marriage Clive had effected Vanessa's defeat on two fronts simultaneously, the one purely sensual and the other intellectual. Truly the admiration of Bloomsbury for the 18th century could have been pushed no further. Even the characters in *Les Liaisons Dangereuses* – one of Clive's favourite masterpieces – were not more completely prostituted.

Vanessa's feelings ran deep, and whether or not she was fully conscious of all the implications, she must have suffered enormously, particularly from jeaslousy of a much loved and cherished sister. Prompted by a natural nobility however, as far as is known she said nothing to either Virginia or Clive. From her own point of view, as well as from theirs, this was a fatal, if charitable mistake. The poison which accumulated, as Virginia later recognised, created a barrier between them which could only be lifted in times of anguish, when Vanessa was at the end of her tether. As for her marriage, although forced by her commitment to the values of Bloomsbury to compound with Clive's infidelity, it was from this moment – that is to say from the outset – that its failure became inevitable.

It is evident from Vanessa's letters to Clive that her attitude to life was, though sensitive and humorous, not passionate otherwise than sexually. Both her ideals and her morals were virtually non-existent, accommodating themselves to circumstances according to her needs of the moment in a way her friends called tolerant. In contrast to her moving feminine beauty and evident sensibility, her reactions to the human predicament were highly critical and, except when they were compulsive, rather indifferent. Bloomsbury called her uncompromising because she was wilful, just as they said she was devastatingly honest when she was occasionally insensitive. She thought she was the most modern and enlightened of wives whereas in reality her attitude was no more evolved than that of Jane Bennet in *Pride and Prejudice.*

The most important result of marriage however was not infidelity but maternity, and Vanessa's consequent absorption in her children occupied her to an unusual degree. She had always felt fated to be a mother and judged it as a necessary stage in her development. Indeed with the exception of Virginia, who on her side had virtually chosen to become one of Vanessa's offspring, Vanessa thought it inevitable for any woman. Not for one moment, in her view, did having children mean she was less of an artist – she was, or tried to be, equally committed to both, *both at the same time.* Such an attitude was neither rational nor intellectual, it was not the outcome of a conscious set of values, nor was it the result of an appraisal of her situation, either artistically or socially. It was something she could not help and therefore assumed was justifiable. This conviction gave her the strength to divide herself between children and art – a schism of which I was deeply aware, and which I might not have accepted so readily had I not also felt that it was inevitable. In those days of course it was comparatively easy: Vanessa had money, servants and – the greatest luxury of all – space; and world population was not the urgent question it is today. In any case she was determined to do what she wanted, seeing in it quite simply a healthy and natural desire which, as a woman, she was entitled to fulfill.

Clive however, though one might say fond of small children on a nursery level, was quite unprepared to put himself out for them. This he conveniently postponed until a later date, leaving Vanessa to organise their juvenile lives. The money which he provided prevented this task from being too onerous, while it allowed him the freedom to enjoy himself. Thus Vanessa was able to lead a double existence, partly devoted to her children and partly to her painting. The third part, well hidden beneath the normal current of life, was a growing understanding that Clive was not only unfaithful but irresponsible. When in 1911 her second son Quentin was ill, Clive showed only a superficial interest, and it was then that Vanessa found herself turning for sympathy to Roger Fry.

Vanessa and Clive had first met him some years before, and were both attracted to him. Thirteen years older than Vanessa, Roger was already married and had two children. Owing to his wife's mental illness his experience of marriage had been tragic, just as his upbringing in a Quaker family had been highly moral, austere and inhibited. If the Stephen family also suffered from inhibition it was to a large extent because Sir Leslie was an introvert, hypersensitive and emotionally self-indulgent. Sir Edward Fry seems on the contrary to have been an extrovert with the ambitions of a scientist, and a mind that was narrow and self-righteous – while his dominating wife successfully prevented her six daughters from getting married. As parents they were definitely something to be escaped from, and as a brilliant younger son Roger lost no time in doing so. He was by 1911 a distinguished critic and connoisseur of art, and had of course just organised the first Post Impressionist Exhibition.

At first Vanessa had felt over-awed by Roger's reputation and authority, but once seen in the humanising light of sympathy over Quentin's illness, he lost his capacity to intimidate, and they began to discover that they both possessed an acute visual sensibility, in his case more knowledgeable and articulate, while in hers it was more expressive – indeed her lack of historical knowledge contributed to her sense of freedom as a painter. In addition they were both sensualists, not only sexually but in every aspect of physical existence. Ostensibly they were both lovers of life:

Vanessa radiated joy in her children, her painting and her friends, and so did Roger. In this he showed greater warmth and vitality than she did however. He never had any difficulty in attracting and forming relationships with people of all kinds, an ability that Vanessa both admired and envied. In his longing to go half-way towards an idea or a human being, Roger almost fell over himself with an enthusiasm that naturally communicated itself to the other person. He was capable of completely forgetting himself – a thing that Vanessa could never do unless in front of her easel. With other people she was so acutely aware of her own short-comings that her approach was always tentative, often cold. She was on the defensive and unwilling to admit it. This was the key to Roger's attraction for her: she could hardly believe in the ease with which he cut through all unnecessary and irksome formality and came to the heart of the matter. Here was ease and luxury – how much more thrilling than the material comforts provided by Clive!

Roger had another quality no less vital, albeit one on which Vanessa also prided herself, and that was the feminine gift of sympathy. In Vanessa's case this took the form of identification with whatever was in question – human being or art – whereas in Roger it took a far more active form, constructive and imaginative. An additional asset as far as human relationships were concerned, it was also this that made him into a great critic.

In 1911 Vanessa, Clive and Roger went to Turkey, where Vanessa fell seriously ill. Clive avoided the sick-room, relinquishing his conjugal rights together with his conjugal responsibilities. These last were assumed almost automatically by Roger, undaunted at having to play the role of hospital nurse to a beautiful woman in the small town of Broussa. His awareness of both her physical and her psychological needs made him the perfect potential lover, father, nurse and doctor rolled into one. Not only did he take her temperature, puff up her pillows and perform the more intimate tasks of the sick-room but, while at other moments continuing to paint, would bring back finds from the market place, talk about Giotto while washing his brushes in her hand basin and leave his palette still covered with colours on her bed while he asked her opinion of his afternoon's work. From her point of view he remained deliciously aware of her need of comfort and support while instinctively and irrepressibly calling for her return to life and participation in the things they most enjoyed together.

By the time they were back in London they were in love, he deeply, she in a maze of mental perspectives and widening horizons where sexuality took on a character of luxurious dependence which exactly suited her then state of mind. For she was not well, and was to suffer for the next two years from a lack of energy and general debility indicating a depression parallel to Virginia's maniacal episodes. Vanessa found herself unable to paint, a condition where Roger's patience and understanding were of inestimable value since he seems to have had faith that, as her health improved her ability to work would again assert itself.

With regard to art, one aspect of great importance was that, although Roger's sights were set high – that is he thought in terms of Giotto, Raphael, Rembrandt and Cézanne – he also embraced with enthusiasm the smallest and least pretentious artistic effort, the anonymous textile or painted box, the odd ceramic or piece of peasant pottery. Thus Vanessa, retreating into childhood after so many years spent as the most responsible member of her family, found herself decorating a hat or making paper flowers with the same seriousness that she would have applied to a picture. This was a therapy which, while it welcomed her back to life, implied a new attitude to art, throwing as it were artist, decorator and craftsman into the same melting pot. In eliminating the barriers that until then had existed between Fine Art and Decorative Art, the artist himself discovered a new freedom in moving from one domain to another according to his own inner necessity: he was no longer bound by the protocol of Fine Art versus Crafts-manship and could lay the same emphasis on each without losing face. This stimulated Vanessa's desire to embellish for example the objects in her house, and though she would probably have respected the identity of an old and valuable piece of furniture, it enabled her to metamorphose the cheap and shoddy into a thing of beauty, even though it might not last for ever. Thus her decorative art was in a sense visionary; it charmed gaiety and vitality out of the air even when the basic material was of the most common and ordinary kind. It is this attitude which enabled the artists of Charleston to treat a piece of furniture or a wall in exactly the same way as a canvas, a new freedom which accounts for its vitality. The painters themselves sometimes expressed it as a dislike of prettiness, a negative way of saying that all objects, including walls, doors and fireplaces, should play a positive part, coming alive in a new context, a new relationship, symbolising life itself.

For all this Vanessa did not cease to be a Fine Artist, not fearing to compare her own work, unfavourably of course, with that of Piero della Francesca or Cézanne, two of the artists she most admired. In spite of the fact that Roger had immeasurably broadened her outlook, she continued to be arrogant and judged the work of her contemporaries without mercy while, in some other compartment of her mind, she admitted that Mr Anonymous had as much right to have his work considered seriously as she had. This was of course a political attitude, and Vanessa was one of the least political of women. Though she subscribed to it in theory she found it very difficult in practice to admit that the artistic gropings of the old lady over the way, or the week-end painter from Cornwall had as much right to consideration as she had. At bottom she tended to despise the amateur; dismissing them with one hand she encouraged them with the other, a double attitude very typical of her and which eventually marred her reputation for generosity, though she did make exceptions, especially for the young with whom she always genuinely sympathised.

In human relationships Vanessa's motives remained mysterious even to Roger. He could not reconcile her evident sensibility and occasional warmth and tenderness with her fundamental indifference. Her physical beauty, allied to a sometimes mischievous sense of humour, suggested a character of sweetness and nobility under which lay great depths of feminine sympathy always liable to qualification by a too arbitrary sense of discrimination. She appeared to make sweeping reservations which, while she kept them to herself, cast a cold shadow even on those with whom she was most intimate. Although she never came out into the open and discussed it, Roger knew that she was deeply critical of his painting, somehow suggesting moral as well as aesthetic disapproval, and causing a pain which she refused to recognise. It was this kind of attitude which gave her an air of ruthlessness, as though on occasion she put on blinkers, and which made her friends, if they loved her, simply stand back and gasp. Her critical faculties amounted really to no more than a bunch of prejudices, never dissolved by analysis. At the same time her fear of emotional confrontation also played its part in preventing her from understanding the effect she had on others. What in the beginning had been an admirable desire to discriminate, had by now become a need to create a magic circle which, excluding those she judged unworthy, included the few she had decided not to judge at all. The distressing part of Roger's situation lay in the fact that he was half out and half in, and although Vanessa imposed her reactions to his art as objective, he knew perfectly well that they were judgments of feeling, which had their roots in something far deeper and less easy to come to terms with. Even he, with his infinitely greater capacity for analysis and objectivity, could not persuade Vanessa to face the enigma with greater honesty, and it seems likely that this area of misunderstanding, all the more threatening for being so vague and ill-defined, was what finally drove a wedge between them. Roger's love continued unabated, becoming ever more demanding the more hurt he felt. It was Vanessa's that cooled, largely because she could not come to terms with her own problems. She had stumbled on important and perplexing questions, but had not solved them: she had inadvertently revealed the fact that she wanted not truth but power, not quality but pre-eminence.

Thus it seems clear that when Duncan emerged from the background to take his place in Vanessa's life, he held a double fascination for her. On the one hand she admired his work without reservation, on the other he became almost automatically a son. A few years earlier Vanessa had spoken of him, from her vantage point of six years seniority, as one of the "most promising and interesting" among the younger artists. The sympathy they soon discovered for each other's work was to take on a new dimension in the light of Post-Impressionism and The Omega Workshops, inspired by Fry, while in their growing intimacy each recognised in the other a sense of humour that was often complementary – Duncan's fantastic and Vanessa's ironic.

There seems to be no consensus of opinion as to when Vanessa and Duncan first became lovers, or what it was that pushed them over the edge of simple companionship into physical intimacy and life-long companionship. I think it is likely that it was Vanessa rather than Duncan who played the role of seducer, tempted among other things by the possibility of success in an emotional area that few other women had apparently attempted. I can see her in a state of almost flippant unbelief, swept off her feet by her eventual triumph. One must remember too that, though an avowed homosexual, Duncan was not indifferent to female charm providing that its owner did not require him to be adult – and this Vanessa never did. When he eventually succumbed to her extraordinary combination of grace and will-power, it was as a blind person setting out to sea on a raft; one may see it as a passive act of surrender, as well as an act of faith.

Duncan's need of Vanessa seemed genuine enough and, within certain well-defined limits, it was. At the same time he was as elusive as an eel, determined to maintain his independence, both with regard to painting and to personal relationships. Other people's deeper needs scarcely impinged on him; he was at bottom quite as indifferent to their demands, in spite of his friendliness and charm, as Vanessa was to their ultimate destiny. While Roger had demanded a maturity which, from her manner, everyone assumed was hers, Duncan had no such aim largely because he was emotionally uninvolved, or involved without perspective, as a child might be.

Duncan had the mysterious attraction of a changeling. He was like a seed blown by the wind with only one root which descended deep into his painting; otherwise he was at the mercy of anyone whose emotional needs were greater than his own. If these became too stringent his equilibrium was threatened, and like the Cheshire Cat, he faded out, leaving nothing but a smile behind him. If he succumbed to Vanessa it was because she was the only woman who combined the sensibilities of the artist with maternal reassurance, within whose arms he found protection and tranquility. He took what he needed and gave what he could: who after all can do more? He never pretended to do or to be other than what he was, never undertook to perform any obligation he knew himself to be incapable of. Like an animal, he was incorruptible.

Those who looked on them from the outside, albeit from a short distance, such as Virginia and Bunny Garnett, saw them as idyllically happy. Concentrated on their painting, fecund in art if not yet in children, they lived on a magic island of which Vanessa was undoubted Queen, able – or almost so – to refuse admittance to anyone she did not like. Isolated not only by the uncertainty of war but by the intransigence of their own attitude towards it, they had discovered a way of life that, apparently unaware and self-indulgent, was also an expression of gentleness in the face of aggression, of the power of passivity when faced by violence and hysteria.

This attitude was visibly reinforced by the amount of work they achieved, in spite of Duncan's commitment as a farm labourer and Vanessa's as a mother and organiser of a household. It is the quality of this work, audacious and life-enhancing, that we so much admire today. If they appear to us as children living in a golden age, they were not sybarites; if they enjoyed such luxuries as space, one or two servants and the joy of intimate communion with each other, they put them to good use. They had no more than enough money and few comforts; their lives were spartan compared with our own. This lack of luxury was undoubtedly stimulating, and certainly played its part in causing them to invent substitutes for things they could ill afford to buy, which they frequently covered with imaginative and spontaneous designs. In these they showed their very different personalities, Duncan's vivacious and witty, Vanessa's cool, balanced and reflective. If she was the moon, Duncan was a star, sometimes shooting erratically across the sky.

From Vanessa's point of view however there was a fly in the ointment: indeed there were two of them, one male and the other female, though they cannot be compared in importance. The first of these was David Garnett who, as everyone now knows, was Duncan's lover and young friend, to whom Duncan was as devoted as he had ever been to anyone. Vanessa decided to compound with his presence in the household, feeling that it was inevitable, and that if she chased Bunny away Duncan would follow him. One may see in her attitude either passion or possessiveness, complaisance or tolerance or more likely an illogical mixture. There was no doubt that she was fond of Bunny for his own sake, and if she suffered from jealousy the inner certainty of her importance for Duncan must have been sufficient to protect her from its worst effects. They all lived together, first in Suffolk and then at Charleston for three years of the War, a time which they each saw much later as couleur-de-rose, and indeed the high-spirited stories which echoed across the dining-room table kept us in fits of laughter for the next twenty years.

The other fly in the ointment was Mary Hutchinson, and if her role, compared with Bunny's, was less intimately bound up with Vanessa's happiness, it was nonetheless illuminating, and was superficially connected with one of the major emotional catastrophes of Vanessa's life. To begin with Vanessa had shown extraordinary self-control in relation to Duncan, so delighted to be his constant companion that she had, one imagines, been a sensitive and undemanding lover. Stimulated in all probability by Bunny's presence in the house, however, this situation insensibly changed. Vanessa's desire strengthened, and in doing so alarmed and terrified Duncan, who only then began to realise that he held in his arms a full-blooded and unsatisfied woman who deep in her heart wanted the impossible. He felt deeply inadequate and, reacting with the direct simplicity of a child, told her he could no longer sleep with her. For him the pain lay in the announcement only, not simply because he had other relationships but because his conscience was clear. His priority was painting; human beings with all their subtleties and complications were peripheral. For Vanessa however it was a blow to the solar plexus from which she never recovered.

In 1918 she was 38; nearly half her life was over. She was about to have a third child by the man – a strangely limited if wonderful being – who had just rejected her. She could not complain that she had been abandoned, since Duncan was outwardly as affectionate and attentive as ever, but she felt alone in life as never before, face to face with the terrifying prospect of taking responsibility for herself. In the past her support for her brother Thoby, for Virginia, and her demonstrations of maternal feeling for Clive, Roger and many of her Bloomsbury friends, had led them all to the assumption that this was indeed what she had done, when in fact her energies had been directed toward taking on responsibility for *them* – a very different state of things.

Each in their own way had resisted, Thoby by dying, Clive and Duncan through unfaithfulness: Virginia alone still burdened Vanessa with her longing for love, and Roger, who had continued to love her, she had herself rejected. Though Vanessa was surrounded by men who professed to adore her, she knew that none of them was prepared to lift a finger to help her, just as on her side she was unwilling to give them their freedom. Clive still hovered in the background, in the habit of going to Charleston for the week-end with his ardently loved mistress, Mary Hutchinson. One might think such a gesture lacking in tact, but for Bloomsbury such a suspicion was unworthy. Vanessa was forced to be reluctantly polite if not welcoming.

Whereas Vanessa was earth-mother and goddess, instinctive rather than intellectual, Mary was highbrow, sophisticated, sociable and elegant; her charm and attraction were based on her ability to use her mind, with which she aimed at keeping up with developments in the artistic world; in addition she was a writer and a salonnière. Vanessa had already painted one portrait of her, now in the Tate Gallery, which shows explicitly what she felt about her, especially if one compares it with a photograph of Mary in real life, a witty juxtaposition made by Frances Spalding in her biography of Vanessa. In 1918 Vanessa started a much bigger canvas called *The Tub,* also in the Tate. It has the mysterious quality of a dream, and clearly demonstrates Vanessa's predicament. To begin with it was to be a composition with Mary as the single figure, dressed simply in a short white shift. But somehow giving the principal role to a woman who was after all her rival, and whose livelier intellect must have recalled Clive's flirtation with Virginia twelve years before felt all wrong and, with the gesture of one who, whatever her failures on the human scene, remained mistress of her own fate on canvas, she painted Mary out – it is interesting to note that it was in relation to Clive rather than Duncan that jealousy raised its head, and triumphed.

In the final version the shift has been removed to reveal a completely nude figure which is obviously a self-portrait. Nudity symbolizes on the one hand a longing for the truth, on the other a revelation of the self in all its vulnerability. She, whom I will now call Vanessa, is contemplating her hands fingering the plait of hair in a gesture which reminds me of someone playing the game of "he loves me, he loves me not". The water in the tub may be seen as the water of life, from which the figure is strangely dissociated. Vanessa had arrived at a parting of the ways, and was deeply troubled.

It is irrelevant to wonder whether Vanessa might have discovered a new way of looking at herself. Judging from *The Tub* she came very near it, which in itself is pretty remarkable. It is probable that she was prevented from a complete revelation by a mere hair's breadth, but it is the hair's breadth which counts; for her the moment of truth contained not only her own personal predicament but her love for Duncan, and it was this rather than independence which won the day. If Bloomsbury on the whole was unsympathetic or suspicious of the workings of the unconscious and unwilling to be helpful, it must also be said that Vanessa, self-sufficient and used to having it all her own way, found it almost impossible to ask for help, and this picture must be regarded as an appeal that, though eloquent, was mute. It went unheeded and she rolled it up and put it under the eaves at Charleston where it lay until it was discovered by Simon Watney 60 years later.

Had it not been for my existence Vanessa and Duncan might I think have drifted apart. But my presence forced Vanessa to reorganise her life once more round the domestic hearth and the nursery, and however little responsibility Duncan assumed, or was allowed to assume, I created a tie which could hardly be brushed aside. Henceforward Vanessa turned towards Duncan in a new attitude of supplication, mutely imploring him not to desert a woman who had after all sacrificed to him something very deep in her nature. She was often jealous, perpetually alarmed that he would leave her but, having outgrown the aura of Demeter, she donned the cloak of Piero's Virgin, and spreading it out warmed us all beneath it. Duncan and Clive had this in common, that they both adored domesticity and Vanessa provided them each with an atmosphere that was mixed exactly to their taste.

Thus as a child I was brought up on the brink of an extinct volcano. The Bloomsbury conception of civilised self-control was largely responsible for what was, psychologically speaking, a very considerable achievement of continuing to live together in harmony while as artists they continued to express some at least of their fantasies. There were, as there always are, tensions: but their triumph consisted in their discovery of how to avoid them, which explains why each person had a room of their own, why the painters occupied one part of the house and the writers another and why, from time to time, both Duncan and Clive absented themselves and went off to gather sustenance in "another part of the forest".

I was the youngest of the family by eight years which, when one is four or five, makes an incalculable difference. My life was regulated in an entirely different way from that of the grown-ups whom I looked on with eyes of wonder and longing – wonder at their seemingly gigantic, shadowy proportions, and longing to be like them and with them since they had a gift for making life tantalisingly exciting, in contrast to the nursery where one had to eat up one's bread and butter and submit to being put to bed just at the moment the lamps were lit and the moths could be seen flitting erratically about the garden. It was the moment when voices changed their timbre, sounding relaxed and self-satisfied after a good day's work. The grown-ups came together rather like animals to the drinking pool, ready to be friendly, ready to snatch at any possibility of enjoyment preferably in the shape of gossip or scandal, ready to sit round the dinner table and relish the conversation without which the salt of life would be missing. From my room above the sitting room I could hear them after dinner going on and on – seldom excited or carried away, unless Virginia happened to be there. Usually however they were very gentle and reflective until someone made a remark – which of course one could never manage to hear – and a burst of laughter would fly out through the french windows, startling the swallows under the eaves, while from the garden a powerful scent of flowers stole into the room. Gradually the myriad sensations of the day would fall away like grains of sand, leaving me high up, cradled by the delicious fatigue of the very young, falling asleep with a sense of unthreatened security.

The extraordinary thing about these strange people was that, no matter what one did or how one behaved, they remained uninvolved – nothing appeared to affect them. Not quite as formidable as the granite figures in Erewhon, who only spoke when the wind whistled through the holes in their faces, they might be likened to trees in the forest whose conversation went on well above one's head, or giant sunflowers, occasionally bending down to see what was going on in the world at their feet. We each had to make a considerable effort to get somewhere near each other's level; nonetheless there was something so fascinating about them that I never ceased to try, and they on their side cultivated an amazing, even an angelic patience only rewarded as far as I know by my present grateful remembrance.

It made a great deal of difference being the only girl – even when I was only three Clive flattered me by every means in his power, repeating my words with unfeigned delight. Maynard Keynes gave me perfumed salts for my bath, Roger Fry made me presents of jewelry, Saxon Sydney-Turner of ornate satin easter eggs for which, as he was so shy and undemanding, I forgot to thank him; everyone who came to the house showered me with presents, some of which I still have. I was treated like a princess; it was not for nothing that I had been named after the Princess Angelica in Thackeray's *The Rose and the Ring*. Although I was not the only girl in the world, I was the only girl in Vanessa's world which like the Ring was a magic circle within which I was the Rose: it was unimaginable to be anything but happy.

Vanessa was the autocrat of this miniature world, ruling it with an absolute authority that the adults respected even if the children occasionally staged a rebellion. Her word was law and had been for so long that we all knew it by heart and made it our own. We lived and breathed by her light, and her presence was felt in every corner of house and garden, and was often both tangible and visible. Who else had put up the wobbly or warped shelves of books, or tied the heavy iron rod to a couple of nails to hang a curtain from? Who else could have made the linen chair covers in the drawing room or sewn the amazing piece of cheap braid all the way round Duncan's bedspread? Who else could have painted the poppies with drooping heads on the panels under the window downstairs, or chosen walls of sooty black and venetian red for her own sleeping chamber? Who else would tackle the Gage Estate about the state of the road, or the Lewes County Council about the rates? Who else could make a panic-stricken Grace go to the doctor for a poisoned thumb, or inspire her to make a hooked rug? And who else indeed could have persuaded Duncan that it would be unwise to have flamingoes on the pond? All these things and many more were attended to by

Vanessa in a spirit of quiet if slightly rueful enjoyment. Nothing ever went completely right and I often think that the angel of improvisation must have sat on her shoulder, always ready to lend a hand to disguise some excess or make up for some short-coming. One of the most important lessons she taught me was that, when you are seriously aiming at the masterwork of your life, and it goes wrong – as it invariably does – there is always a remedy at hand, and one must never be too proud to use it. She never was herself, although I well remember, when the crisis arrived, her cry of horror and the way her hand, sometimes holding a paint brush, flew to her head in a gesture which recalled that of the man who closed the stable door after the horse was stolen.

Though I feel strongly that after 1918 Vanessa's life ceased to be even nominally independent, since she had bound herself to Duncan by means that were too disingenuous to be recognised for what they were, yet her vitality was so strong that she was able to persuade those around her, including herself, that she was happy. Though she had said goodbye to freedom, she maintained a creative capacity which surpassed that of most people. The eye of the painter remained to endow her pictures with a luminous subtlety that increased with age and experience. The self-por-traits she painted at the very end of her life are remarkable for their insight, and for the feeling they give of philosophical acceptance of what she saw as a hard destiny as well as a continuing pleasure in the sensuousness of colour and paint. The passage of time did for her what she could not do for herself and by its own mysterious processes reassembled what had been dissociated, making an impressive whole out of a life that had been extraordinarily rich and variegated.

II

Duncan

In 1990 John Maurray published a book by Simon Watney about my father Duncan Grant and I was asked by Karen Wright, of *Modern Painters*, to write not so much a review of the book as an article on Duncan himself. This meant that Simon's work got insufficient attention, and I would like to make amends here by saying that this is the only monograph to date that takes Duncan's painting seriously. The text is both thoughtful and illuminating. In spite of certain reservations I have about the illustrations, which have not always been chosen to represent Duncan at his best, it remains a valuable contribution to our knowledge of Duncan as an artist, his relations to his period, and indeed to our understanding of English art of the twentieth century.

Duncan is often in my mind. I think of him, trying to understand all he meant for me, and to situate him in the world that, though of different generations, we both shared. I have taken my original article as a peg on which to hang nothing very new, using it as an opportunity to indulge in one of my favourite pastimes, that of reflection on a much loved and never to be exhausted subject.

Born in 1885 actually at Rothiemurchus, on the Spey, Duncan passed much of his childhood in India and Burma, a fact which appeared almost literally to colour his life as though, still very young, he had been dipped by the Great Agrippa into a bottle of India Ink not, however, necessarily black. He had an ayah of whom he was very fond and, at one time, an English nurse who meant a lot to him. An only child, he was doted on by his mother and loved I think to a more reasonable degree by his military, musical and botanist father Bartle, member of an ancient Scottish family and brother of Lady Strachey, whose children were therefore Duncan's cousins. When Bloomsbury came into existence Duncan was, although at the time an almost unknown quantity, inevitably included.

As a child Duncan started painting, very possibly because, in spite of mother, ayah or nurse, he was lonely, but much more, I like to think, because, naturally sensuous, he responded spontaneously to what he saw – bedizened elephants, boats in the harbour and the rich and astonishing colours of the East. He painted a number of pictures which he gave as a mark of affection to his nurse, some of which I remember having seen shortly after his death in the studio at Charleston. I was aware of their happy precocity and gaiety and the fact that, with hindsight, one could recognise their affinity with Duncan's later work. Simon reproduces two of them in his book.

Duncan was a biddable and happy child, neither rebellious or cantankerous. I think he would agree with my feeling that painting was for him a gift from God, the pursuit of which kept him alive. It was this conviction which necessitated a certain detachment from the inexplicable quagmires of emotional relationships and which made him seem, at times, like a transient being from another world. Never harsh or insensitive, never apparently taken unawares, he was a past master of eluding what I suppose many people would call responsibility. But it is only too easy for those who see life in terms that are predominantly moral – a question of oughts and shoulds – to dismiss a man of Duncan's 'lightness of being' in a way that misses the entire point of his personality. It is possible to say that he was irresponsible in having a child he was not prepared to cherish as his own, but it is also possible to see such reluctance as a measure of Duncan's dedication to his art. At least, as far as I can make out, he never lied about it and although, as a result of his comparative indifference I suffered deeply, I would not wish to change a hair of Duncan's head. There was something impervious in his nature, something buoyant and unjudgmental, that made such moral considerations seem entirely irrelevant. I find it impossible to regard him as an example of iniquity, perhaps because I am too cowardly or perhaps because, like my mother, I was too much in love with him to see him with any detachment. But Vanessa must not be forgotten, nor her determination to have and to take charge of me when I arrived on the scene. For her, possibly to a greater extent that she realised, I was a part of Duncan, the part she could most easily possess, but whose existence, she decided, must not be allowed to impinge on his professional life. Theirs was not the normally shared life of a couple, at least not in this respect, and in view of their personalities and preoccupations it is hard to see how it could have been otherwise.

If my mother was possessive it was partly because she imagined herself obliged to take charge. But Duncan showed no hurt pride – he was the least competitive of men. Although he was incapable of supplying my deeper emotional needs as a daughter, he showed both interest and affection for me and my development. The delight of being with him lay in the fact that he never tried to teach an unwanted lesson, that he had no axe to grind. He allowed me, as he did everyone else, complete liberty of action. He never bossed anyone around, never tried to take possession of them, and did not manipulate them. If they did not understand him and his very simple needs, he did not raise a warning finger or put out a hand to stop the progress of events. In love

37

affairs he might suffer, might burst into tears or become grumpy, betraying his fragility and infantilism. But he never behaved resentfully or with animosity.

Duncan and my mother were bound together by a deep loyalty and affection that outweighed all else, containing the sort of happiness that comes from a long enduring intimacy, even though that intimacy contained moments of anguish, particularly for her, both communicable and, sometimes, inexpressible. Looking back, I see their emotional relationship and their artistic partnership as inextricably mixed, although they themselves attempted to believe otherwise. Perhaps it would be truer to say that Vanessa, while always feeling deeply, tried hard to be rational, whereas Duncan could not be otherwise than instinctive, and relied on her judgment in all respects. They appeared to think themselves tremendously objective about their painting, but were not so I think more than about anything else. When Duncan found himself confronted by a problem, he suffered acutely, to be comforted, in technical terms, by Vanessa who, while doubting her own adequacy as a critic, responded with all the sensitivity and honesty characteristic of her. But she was too close to Duncan, too aware of his need of spiritual support, and too dyed with the colours of Roger Fry's mind, to be sufficiently stimulating. Her very integrity was forbidding, her influence too moral, carrying with it all the emotional weight of a maternal, protective presence which, because of her vulnerability, could never be disputed without giving pain. And yet each was magnetized by the other because of their capacity for creating something that was unforeseen and original, giving them the magic power to produce a world of their own.

Charleston, the nucleus of this world, is still available for the visitor to see that it was never thought of by the artists as a mere framework to show themselves off, or indeed as a showcase for its contents. It was a private creation, more like a meditation which changed and expanded over the years, spontaneous and intimate.

It was, however, only one aspect of their lives, the other being their life in London, more public and more sociable. Until sometime in the early thirties we lived at N° 37 Gordon Square, where the size of the house, its large, decorated double drawingroom on the first floor, its long windows draped and dappled from without by the plane trees in the Square, lent an attractive gentility to our lives that had more to do with the nineteenth than the twentieth century. This feeling was increased by the fact that there was no studio or working area. It was the nearest that Duncan and Vanessa ever came to living like a lady and gentleman. The fact that Maynard Keynes lived a few doors further on and the Strachey family almost at the end of the row, that Clive had his bachelor flat in between and that Virginia and Leonard lived just around the corner gave it the character of an enclave, a private precinct within which communication was delightfully easy although, at the same time, individual liberties were scrupulously respected. Our servants too were on terms of friendship with each other, and provided a sort of grass roots system which tended to consolidate the fabric of our daily existence.

By 1928 Vanessa and Duncan had found studios at N° 8, Fitzroy Street, to which they went every day after breakfast, rather as businessmen depart for their offices. A year or two later the house in Gordon Square was given up and they occupied their studios full time. Here I think they found life both easier and more congenial for, although it was only a few streets away, the atmosphere of Fitzroy Street was quite different. Instead of the plane trees and green lawns of the Square there were pubs and restaurants, interspersed with the blackened brick facades of Georgian houses and hardware shops just round the corner. Behind Vanessa's studio, on a lower floor, there was Mr Ferro, a skilful Italian woodcarver who would turn his hand to anything. And in front of the house there was Drown's, framers and picture restorers. Everything was incredibly shabby, the front hall cold and dark. Standards of gentility hardly existed. In such a setting Vanessa became even more imposing, whereas Duncan fitted in, as though born to it, having made friends with many people in the vicinity. He occupied a studio that had previously been Whistler's whereas Sickert had at one time owned or worked in Vanessa's and had left a small picture in the coal hole which, once rescued, she hung on the wall at Charleston. Here every day at about 6.0 in the evening Flossie would arrive, a gaunt and rather forbidding figure who cooked in the morning for Helen Anrep in Charlotte Street, and in the evening for Vanessa. Our meals were very English, hardly *cordon bleu* but adequate, accompanied by red wine in pale blue glasses with square pedestals, bought at Heal's.

Vanessa's studio was a queer mixture of dust and grandeur, dimly lit by a huge window revealing shadowy depths full of paint boxes, easels and canvasses. The walls were of greenish match boarding, in front of which was to be seen the usual still life of fruit and flowers, gradually losing its colour as, scrupulously untouched, it was 'gone on with' day after day. The Pither stove warmed the painting half of the studio, its huge space ostensibly divided by two splendid appliqué curtains made by Vanessa and brought from Gordon Square, which hung from an iron rod suspended from wall to wall. On the hither side of this division was Vanessa's bed, serving often as a sofa, and a gas fire under a small mantelpiece, over which hung a tarnished mirror adding a dim gleam of light to this domestic corner. Round the table were Omega chairs, of a glowing sealing-wax red, enlivening the somewhat somber tones that prevailed. There was a separate lavatory, but the bath was in the kitchen, the water heated by a potentially explosive but efficient geyser. I would often have

40

my bath before supper when Flossie was busy at the stove cooking our meal, and we would sometimes watch the feet of Duncan's guests as they passed the little window which looked onto the passage leading to his studio.

This, the same as Vanessa's but in reverse, reflected his own personality. There were one or two comfortable chairs in front of a gas stove, a small sideboard stocked with bottles and, on one side, the little square piano by Jacob Kirckman, at which Mrs Hammersley sat for her portrait. But most of the space was given over to painting, with the classic paraphernalia of the nineteenth century artist, a model's throne and a screen, quantities of brushes standing in pots and a long mirror. A similar huge window shed over everything a cold north light. At the back, instead of a kitchen there was a small bedroom.

Duncan was no doubt ambitious, but unworldly, and his aim – to devote himself to his art – singularly pure. This did not mean that he did not welcome success, when it occurred, but it enabled him to divest himself of any peripheral interests, even amorous ones, leaving the centre of his life uncorrupted. His art sprang from his vision of life as a continual orgy of looking and seeing. His imagination teemed with possibilities of an exotic nature constantly demanding expression. In order to give reality to such a vision he created his own surroundings, and lived both in and with them, changing and recording them as both he and they changed with time. Either in Fitzroy Street or at Charleston he could maintain a running conversation between past and present, a past that, often reflected in mirrors, was repeated and transformed into a new present. One illuminated the other, such as, in *Moments of Being* and other writing, Virginia Woolf was also to do.

A constantly pursued sensuality is an emotional state, a climate of the mind. Sensuality is an essential element in all his

41

work and is, I think, the most obvious distinction between him and other twentieth century English artists. Only Mathew Smith felt things with such warm immediacy. Duncan's visions, although erotic and even, on occasion, pornographic, were not voyeuristic, and contain nothing that you could suspect of trying to teach you a lesson. Instead, he creates a world you are free or not to enter, one springing directly from his own pleasure in creating it. If he never appeals to emotion in the raw it was not because he was an unfeeling man but because he thought that art is designed to please and refresh. Often teased by Clive and Virginia for his lack of book learning, he was a cultivated artist who had learned a lot from study of the old masters, with whom he kept up a constant dialogue. A sensitive and inventive colourist, he was also a remarkable draughtsman who thought of drawing as the basis of art. It was to this that he returned when the extraordinary excitement of Post Impressionism subsided. While it provided him with an undeniable security in creating a link between his own work and that of the great painters he so much admired, it came to be seen more and more as an academic point of view which created a barrier between him and the new avant garde such as Benedict Nicholson. He was however perfectly capable of admiring Nicholson or such painters as Braque or Kandinsky without wishing to follow in their footsteps.

Quentin criticized Duncan, with some truth, for lack of discrimination in his too frequent appreciation of other artists. But Quentin was a thinker, constantly adjusting his own point of view in a historical perspective, whereas Duncan was a lover whose affections were stimulated by simple sincerity. With the exception of the truly vulgar almost anyone who had put paint on canvas aroused his sympathy, and his innate loyalty led him to defend, not only Delacroix and Burne-Jones, frowned on by Vanessa, but academic artists of the nineteenth century laughed at unconditionally – and perhaps unfairly – by the rest of us. Art sometimes seemed like a hilly landscape with some mountains from which you could get a marvellous view, and others it was hardly worth the trouble of climbing. But for Duncan it was mostly a delight, a country in which he spent most of his life.

Duncan's charm, marvelled at almost excessively by his friends, remains difficult to define. Outwardly his manner was perfectly self-possessed and dignified. It belonged to an age when formality and reserve were considered estimable qualities, and politeness in all normal transactions was taken for granted. Duncan was naturally gentle and, although capable of salty and even subtle repartee, he was never over quick or brilliant. He usually reflected well before he spoke, and said no more than was necessary, but this in itself often seemed to us full of originality. His accounts of his experiences while absent from home which, as a much appreciated guest, he often was, were brief and pithy. He never indulged, like Virginia, in flights of fantasy.

And yet it was obvious that he lived in a world of his own. Objects and their relationships seen in the changing light of the sun or, ambiguously, at night, lost their every day meaning and became almost purely abstract. But if he saw them in terms of colour and shape, light and shadow, he also delighted in their objective existence, their individual significance, which he instinctively respected. This attitude, also evident in his human relationships, was something he could not help, that gave him a very special aura and was, perhaps, at the root of his charm. I am sure it was this which prevented the young men from the Navy, longing for revenge after the supposed indignity of the Dreadnought Hoax, from beating him to a jelly. And it was this same respect for identity which made him save a single mouse from death at the hands of farm labourers and their threshing machine when he was a conscientious objector. There was nothing sentimental about it: he simply acted in response to his own nature, never dramatising and seldom repining, indeed more often than not laughing, both at the situation, and at the role he had played in it. He neither took himself too seriously nor denied his right to exist, and cannot be accused, as the rest of Bloomsbury often is, of arrogance. He should probably have stood up for himself more than he did. But if this was a fault, it appealed to his friends, who were always ready to help him.

On an occasion such as the painful encounter with D.H. Lawrence, or when his animosity towards Herbert Read or John Rothenstein rose to the surface, it was not so much that their opinions were unacceptable, although this was an important ingredient, as that there was something in their personalities and behaviour to which Duncan reacted emotionally, as animals do for reasons we can only guess at. Not that Duncan would bite – but he would growl, and then retire from the scene, without explanation. Unlike some, perhaps most, of the members of Bloomsbury, including to a certain extent Vanessa, Duncan was not fond of analysing his own or other people's behaviour. He preferred a metaphor or a joke, or the single, telling word which, in dealing economically with the subject, restored order and a sense of proportion. In love he could no doubt suffer from jealousy, but he was never resentful or spiteful and, although sometimes called the Bear, he never, in my experience, lost his temper.

Unlike Vanessa, Duncan did not dream of total privacy in which to work, and after her death he became freer, at Charleston, to entertain all kinds of visitors. If any of these showed the slightest desire to paint, Duncan would provide them with the necessary equipment, and without fuss settle down to share a still life with them. Nothing could be more delightful than to find oneself accepted into a household that, redolent of the past as it was, might otherwise have seemed rather overwhelming. Such relationships, casual and temporary although they often were, could not have worked so well had not Duncan been so unselfconscious, so completely absorbed in what he was doing, and so gentle and undidactic. An interest in painting was taken for granted: what could be more natural than to try one's hand? It was the pleasure that mattered. The unpredictability of the results only made them more interesting, and led to jokes and laughter, never damaging and sometimes illuminating.

With Vanessa no longer there to protect him, Duncan's tolerance, which some regarded as indiscriminate, led much younger people to take advantage of him, sponging on his generosity, filling the house with a restless egocentricity that seemed to have little to do with Duncan's own sensibilities. Nothing however made him depart from his innate dignity, or deflected him from his preoccupation with painting. While others did what they liked he maintained a delicate independence, deriving at the same time considerable amusement from their behaviour.

Duncan's seriousness about art, in providing him with the anchorage he needed, allowed him to laugh as much as he pleased. He often giggled, never roared or shrieked, but occasionally died, to be reborn, wiping tears from his cheeks with his bandanna. He did not indulge in insinuation or slander although he appreciated the wit, however devilish, when Virginia did so. Even then, his comments tended to take the sting out of what had been said, made it no less amusing, and caused no one any harm. He never reproached, blamed or attacked anyone. If he did not like what they said, he avoided them. He never indulged in the orgiastic whipping up of emotion. When anxious or worried he became crusty, obstinate and contradictory. But his growls were essentially anodyne, only asking for gentle treatment, which he rewarded by an effort to control himself.

In spite of Duncan's capacity to respond to the demands and pleasures of the moment, it would be a mistake to think of him as superficial. True, he was neither an intellectual nor a thinker. His art and his actions were guided by intuition, but his empathy and insight allowed him to see far below the surface. He was aware of what was going on in other people and listened to them with sympathy and detachment, unwilling to meddle or interfere.

In spite of his simplicity he was not naîf although, when bored, he could pretend to be. When left to himself however he was never bored, since he always remained in touch with his surroundings. His feeling for objects – a pot, a pencil, a piece of textile or a plant – was in itself almost tangible. The absorption with which he looked at things, the gentleness of his gestures, betrayed their importance for him, as though he were engaged in a secret conversation in which he alone knew the language.

On coming into the studio at Charleston after breakfast, I would find Duncan if not yet already at work, then preparing palette, brushes, painting rag, oil and turpentine to his liking. This he did very quietly and efficiently, probably talking at the same time of something quite different. Work would start at about ten, if not before, and continue until almost one o'clock, with a pause for yet another cigarette, a moment to look at the newspaper and to sit by the stove. In the presence of a model the atmosphere would be a shade less calm, since he could never paint unless the sitter was reasonably happy and comfortable. This induced him to make an effort at conversation, although the radio was often used as a substitute.

Sometimes pictures went wrong, notably when they were of the human figure. One such was a huge canvas of gymnasts or wrestlers which stood for years in the middle of the studio, too large to hide or ignore. Duncan altered and changed it to no avail. It seemed to have the devil in it, representing effort and failure – a daily nightmare. After his death I destroyed it – a blameworthy act no doubt, but a sort of exorcism.

But when Duncan became interested by a new idea he would often start drawing on odd pieces of paper with a 4B pencil, a cigarette hanging from his lip and an air of preoccupation which protected him from any enquiry. With amazing rapidity, mythical figures, animal or human, would spring to life on the page. From this he might proceed to pinning up large pieces of paper on which he would trace his ideas in charcoal with his usual graceful, dance-like gestures. Later in the process he would bring out his stores of coloured papers and, cutting them into shapes, pin them to his design, a technique he used for the Queen Mary panels. At these moments he was completely immersed in what he was doing and perfectly happy. Caught in the midst of such bliss by the telephone or the cook, he remained unfazed, returning to his work without a hair turned.

When Duncan was away, life became dull. When he was present it took on a special radiance, and became twice as worth living. Simply by being himself he conferred magic on the most ordinary acts of everyday life. In his company a mere walk round the garden became a stroll in wonderland because of the quality of his observation. With age, he became more and more of a contemplative, losing himself in what he saw with a sort of rapt awareness of the mystery of existence. Even as a very old man he remained alert, receptive and alive, bathing everyone near him in the glow of his affection.

III

Virginia and Vanessa

Asked to write about Virginia, the best approach seems to be through my mother Vanessa. These two Vs, angular and ambiguous, undecided whether to symbolize V or U. Both sisters started life with the same initials, V.S., then one changed to V.W., a variant on the original, the other to V.B., a round and solid addition. When I see V.B. on the registration plate of a car it immediately causes me a tremor of recognition. V.W. never seems to occur in such places.

Vanessa was the more practical, the more solid, the earthier of the two sisters. Virginia always said so, and the difference must have been marked even when they were young. Vanessa was the elder, a social success, married first and had children. She could mix colours, stretch canvases, cook meals and deal with unpalatable situations. She had a feminine capacity for listening tolerantly to the arguments and ideas of the men they both knew. This made a special place for her in the heart of Bloomsbury. Men from college, used to the freedom of masculine society or the polite and inconsequential chatter of their mothers and sisters, found it delightful to be listened to by a madonna with a sense of humour – a little wild perhaps and original, a little *sans façons* – how piquant it was and, in the end, how

49

restful to be surrounded by a feminine atmosphere without the false obligations created by convention.

Virginia, on the contrary, was shy and awkward, often silent or, if in the mood to talk, would leap into fantasy and folly and terrify the innocent and unprepared. This combination of limpid beauty and demon's tongue proved fatal to those who were too timid to respond and who, ensnared while unconscious, woke like Bottom to find themselves in a fairyland echoing with malicious laughter.

Virginia remained always capable of demolishing the unwary: it was too easy for her, and it was a temptation that sometimes proved irresistible. Like many people who make inordinate demands, Virginia had much to give; if she sometimes wounded her friends they forgave her and came back to her for her quality, the purity of which fascinated so many different people. It was like a diamond stream of water, hard and scintillating, transparent, bubbling, austere and life-giving.

When I knew her best, age and experience had softened her and lit her with a more tender light. She always looked vulnerable – those shadowy temples over which stretched a transparent skin showing threads of blue; the wrinkled waves of her high, narrow forehead; the tautness of those sardonic lips pulled downwards at the corner; her bladed nose, like the breastbone of a bird or the wing of a bat, surmounted by deeply hooded melancholy grey-green eyes. She had the worn beauty of a hare's paw.

Like all the Stephens she was sad in repose – it seemed their most natural attitude – and yet the slightest ripple round her would cause a lightning-flicker in her eye, a flare of sympathy and intelligence. She was a great teaser and a shameless flatterer, avid for affection from those she loved. She adored nicknames: calling Vanessa Dolphin, herself Billy Goat or The Goat, I was Pixerina, Leonard was Leo – and so on. Virginia invented an extra personality for us, a luxury which we enjoyed but which half irritated, half amused, making us appear wonderfully changed as in a fairground mirror.

Virginia's version of Vanessa tended to soar into the Olympic regions, where she subconsciously felt that Nessa belonged. Like a highly coloured transparency held over the original design, sometimes it corresponded, sometimes not. She magnified the importance of Vanessa's practical abilities out of all relation to reality. It was true that Virginia could not bring herself to mend her clothes and preferred to pin up her silk rags with a gold brooch; but she could cook, and bottle fruit – well do I remember the pride she took in her cupboard of jade-green gooseberries and sad-purple raspberries on the stairs at Monks House. She also had a gift for appearance: the interiors of her houses were cool and civilized, the colours muted but various. There was in them nothing planned or self-conscious, though she was discriminating in her choice of objects and furniture. Leonard said that she saw things in antique shops from the window of the car which were nearly always worth stopping for.

Vanessa's strength lay in her closeness to reality, to the everyday world. By comparison she was calm, like a pool on which the coloured leaves slowly change their pattern. She accepted, rather than protested; was passive, rather than avid. She did not care deeply about abstract ideas, and was led by her sensibilities rather than her intellect. In theory she supported rationalism, though her own acts were usually compulsive. She instinctively limited her life to the two things she cared for most: her painting and her family. The wider world seemed to her to threaten these two points, and she appeared to choose the limits of her affection and sympathies. Love, with her, was an exclusive rather than an inclusive emotion: there was a chosen circle round which was planted a high palisade that cast its shadow both on those without and those within.

To Virginia, I think, Vanessa seemed at times formidable,

embodying the spirit of justice and authority inherited from her Stephen ancestors. Virginia danced round her like the dragon-fly round the water-lily, darting in to attack and soaring away before Vanessa could take action. Vanessa had a kind of stoical warmth about her, a monolithic quality that reminded one now of the implacable smile of primitive Aphrodite, now of the hollow wind-whistling statues of Erewhon. She sat and sewed or painted or listened; she was always sitting, sometimes at the head of the table, sometimes by the fire, sometimes under the apple tree. Even if she said little, there emanated from her an enormous power, a pungency like the smell of crushed sage. She presided, wise yet diffident, affectionate and a little remote, full of unquenchable spirit. Her feelings were strong, and words seemed to her inadequate. She was content to leave them to her sister and to continue painting. Virginia's attitude was far from sitting, it was striding; long narrow thighs and shins in long tweed skirts, loping over the Downs, across the water-meadows, beside the river, or through the traffic in London, under the trees in the park and round the square. She was never placid, never quite at rest. Even when, knees angular under the lamp and cigarette in holder, she sat with a friend after tea, she quivered with interest in the doings of other people.

Leonard kept Virginia on very short purse-strings, allowing her so much pocket money a week. This she was free to spend as she chose, though she referred to her dependence in teasing, bantering terms. Since she had to count the shillings, she was more conscious of the pleasure they could bring. She adored shopping as much as any child and was ready to fall for the temptations of coloured string and sealing-wax, notebooks and pencils. We would visit Kettle's shop in New Oxford Street and supply ourselves with printed paper, glue and paper-clips, and sniff the curious smell of dust and brown paper. It was not unlike the smell of Virginia's writing-room in the basement of Tavistock Square, where she sat by the gas fire, surrounded by parcels of books and walls of paper. I did not go to see her there often. Usually I went upstairs, where we amused ourselves by making paper dolls and throwing lumps of sugar out of the window to the cart-horses. Enormously generous, Virginia when she became richer would pile presents on Vanessa and on me. As I grew older these took the form of clothes, and the afternoons spent in this way were less happy. The shop assistants made her feel shy and out of place, and she did not know how to say that a dress did not suit me or what to do about it, so we generally ended with some uneasy compromise relieved by the knowledge that we would soon be going home to tea and Chelsea buns.

The two families, Bells and Woolfs, met frequently. In London they saw each other on Sundays at Clive Bell's flat in Gordon Square; in the summer there were week-end tea parties held either at Monks House or at Charleston. There, if the weather was fine, tea was brought into the garden. Nessa presided at a very low table, while Virginia and Clive teased each other from the depths of Rorky chairs which squeaked when they moved. Clive was relaxed and reflective, puffing his pipe with pleasure, his clothes clean but old. Virginia often wore a hat, and somehow combined elegance with angularity of movement. She seemed more subdued, more observant at Charleston than at Monks House where she herself was hostess. There we always had tea in the dining-room which was sunk below the level of the garden, and dimly green like a fish-pond. Indeed there was an aquarium in the corner which I would stop to look at as Leonard's shaking hands scattered ants' eggs for the fish to eat; they would swim lazily to the surface to swallow, reject and swallow again with apparent indifference. The plants on the window-sills cast a green light into the room, and through their interstices the legs and feet of late or unexpected visitors could be seen arriving. Here Virginia waved her cigarette with infectious excitement and embarked on fantasies which made us hilarious. We egged her on until Leonard punctured her sallies with a sardonic comment, or the flat statement that what she was saying was completely untrue. Then we would troop into the garden for the ritual game of bowls.

Apart from these family invasions the atmosphere of Monks House was concentrated, quiet and mysterious. Pen and ink replaced brushes and turpentine and there were no manual occupations, except for Leonard's gardening. Often when one arrived he would emerge from the bushes in shirt-sleeves, with clay on his boots and a pair of sécateurs in his hand. Then we would go together in search of Virginia, to be found reading in or near her garden-room under the chestnut trees by the churchyard. Their chief amusement was conversation, and many different kinds of people came and went; the house was like a sea-shell through which the water flows, leaving behind it a taste of salt.

There were many occasions when I went to see Virginia alone with Vanessa, and I amused myself while they enjoyed what they called a good old gossip. The intimacy of those occasions remains with me, and leads me to envy the relations between sisters. They understood each other perfectly and were probably at their best in each other's company. They were bound together by the past, and perhaps also by the feeling that they were opposite in temperament and that what one lacked she could find only in the other.

IV

Nursery Days

Was there ever a proper nursery at Charleston? I do not think so, and yet I'm almost sure I didn't always have my meals with the grown-ups. Sometimes in the kitchen with Grace, Louie, Lottie and perhaps others. Hot, steamy and dark, even in summer the kitchen range was alight: Lottie made it roar, manipulating the iron rings in the top. I saw orange circles and glimpsed white heat. Hungry from our walk we sat at the square table and ate slice after slice of white bread and butter, drinking milk from the farm. Louie sat on the edge of her chair and kept us under her eye: in the dining room she could do nothing about our manners, but in the kitchen we must behave ourselves. At the same time she was protective; volatile Lottie must not be allowed to alarm us. I loved Louie, but Lottie was more fascinating. She was a foundling, and that was why she was called Hope. No one knew her real name. She had been left in a cradle on the doorstep of the Hospital, where they had taken her in and looked after her. She had fuzzy hair like a Golliwog's, and her legs were elegant, like those of Mistinguett. Her strap shoes sounded on the kitchen floor almost as though she was tap-dancing in her swinging, pleated skirt. Sometimes her nose looked very red, and she scrubbed it with her pocket handkerchief as though it itched.

55

Where did I hear a rumour that she kept a bottle of whisky in her bedroom? and sometimes lost her temper with violence? When the house caught fire it was she who noticed the smell, and, very excited, ran and told Vanessa. The beam was smouldering and, it seemed, had been burning for weeks. Lottie was a person of extremes; she got up first in the morning to rake out the fire and start it going again, and it seemed as though it melted all the fat off her, and left her, thin and dark, dancing energetically over her saucepans. She was full of laughter, mostly scatty, and strange superstitions jostled in and out of her head, causing Nessa to sigh, after ordering dinner in the morning after breakfast. Having done her best to pour cold water on Lottie's notions, she always discovered that, by the following day, they had returned. One of them was that we liked hot fruit cake, black with raisins and currants and hurriedly iced with thick, soft icing into which she stuck shining red cherries, reminding one of globules of stained glass. Even when we unkindly sent the cake back to the kitchen, saying it was too fresh, we produced only brief discouragement. The following week another would appear, until Vanessa, in some ways the most easy-going of housekeepers, would exclaim at Lottie's extravagance, and discover extra packets of cherries and pounds of currants at the back of the kitchen cupboard.

It was not Lottie however, but an anonymous cook, who came only for the holiday, who overpowered us with jellies. She was the jelly cook par excellence, and discovered in a corner some genteel glass dishes which she filled with the quivering jujube-like mixture in red, yellow and green. Neither lunch nor dinner nor tea was complete without them, and nothing we said changed her conviction that we loved them. We were left with the impression that she had a limited mind – but she must have thought the same of us.

Once I had grown old enough to be allowed to stay up for dinner, each evening became a festive occasion for which, after a day spent getting covered with paint, or mud in the River Ouse, I bathed in the cramped and primitive bathroom, and changed into something which, whatever it looked like, felt like an evening dress. Nessa too changed, and wore long hanging earrings given her by Roger. She looked more beautiful than ever, but her manner, calm and sedate, remained the same.

No matter what Clive did he was always clean – indeed one could only imagine him touching something dirty with hands protected by gloves or a handkerchief. He did not change his clothes for dinner, but brought with him a sense of occasion, a need to find excitement somewhere. I and a friend were the 'young ladies' – what had we been 'up to' all day? He supposed this and that, and with a subtle smile attributed to us all sorts of witty and delightful things we had never thought of. He commanded the conversation, and, having satisfied our longing to be taken notice of, turned his attention to someone else. Perhaps he would call Duncan 'the Colonel', a gambit which enraged Duncan, and made him rub his nose between finger and thumb, trying to think of an adequate answer – an effort which left him laughing, helpless in the face of an attack which seemed to have neither rhyme nor reason. His own contribution to the conversation, always personal, would be an account of some brush with authority in Lewes, or an unforeseen reaction to some well-known work of art, to which he had 'come round', after subjecting it to years of neglect. This would start the sort of conversation that Clive loved, in which he could show off both his erudition and his sophistication, though he was never unmindful of Duncan's originality. There was a deep bond – more than a modus vivendi – between them, on which Vanessa, on the other side of the table, looked with a slightly envious but detached amusement. She seldom joined in unless directly appealed to, when, if a work of art was in question, her reactions were almost maddeningly vague. She hated to commit herself, and yet all seemed to her very obvious –

57

her mind was already made up and had been years and years ago. It was unlikely that, on such an important subject, she would have changed it.

Julian, partly enjoying things as they were, and partly longing to bring in the revolution and turn everything topsy-turvy, couldn't help introducing politics – local perhaps, but just as red to a bull as any others, indeed more so. Though Clive would try to keep his temper, still he had to have his say, at some length, while Julian fidgeted on his chair in total disagreement, which at length burst forth in a kind of squeal, Julian raising his hand, though not quite bringing it down on the table as a fist. Occasionally Nessa's cool voice intervened . . . but usually the intense emotions were battened down, controlled under hatches: the dinner, the evening were what counted.

It was Quentin who brought a leavening of objectivity into these exchanges; thoughts that had occurred to no one else went deeper, further back, made connections, suave, considered, intellectual and just as erudite as Clive's. Delighted, everyone leant back and sipped their wine while Vanessa carved the bird or helped the syllabub.

After the meal I was sometimes put through a questionnaire on the history of England, supposed to help my schooling, but more often I sang songs to my own accompaniment, while the gentlemen smoked cigars and drank brandy. Sometimes I simply flirted with my brothers or other guests – whatever I did I was outrageously spoilt, my ego outrageously administered to; and that is, probably, the main explanation of my character.

V

Reading Aloud

When I think of London in the 1920s with its high, shadowy ceilings and Victorian basements, its linoleum covered stairs and infinite stretches of York paving stones running beside iron railings, it spells gloom and the implied and, for me alien, demand for good behaviour. There were dancing classes in Hampstead, piano lessons in St John's Wood or tea parties at the Raverats', to which I walked or went on the bus with Louie, my nurse, dressed in coat, hat, scarf and gloves, with shoes polished and socks tightly drawn up. The effort to look the same was great but the result, I knew, was inferior to that of the other little girls encountered on such occasions. Delight in the spontaneous sensuality of life was inhibited by the conformity inherent it seemed in the bricks and mortar, the busy roads and eternal noise of London.

The appeal was, and more or less had to be, to the mind rather than to the senses, and mine was sluggish, resisting Rose Paul's effort to teach me arithmetic and spelling in her neat, shining but somehow alien schoolroom in Mecklenburgh Square. I shone, frailly, only when required to recite poetry or draw from life a highly treasured pottery eagle that stood on her mantlepiece. These moments of self-fulfilment were crowned with cosy success, when the three mothers, Mrs Nelson, Gwen Raverat and

Vanessa, refreshed and supported by cups of tea, sat on the small sofa under the window, listening to their three daughters' performance of such poems as 'I remember, I remember, the house where I was born . . .' which epitomised for me my nostalgic craving for Charleston.

When it was at length time to go there it was the arrival and not the journey that mattered, knowing as we did that it was a beginning to long weeks of summer holidays – day after day of pleasurable, even ecstatic sensations untrammeled, or almost, by the oughts and shoulds of convention. Louie fought her own battle for behaviour but, under the umbrella protection of the grown ups, I could often afford to disregard it. Feet went bare, hair unbrushed, and my skimpy frocks were as often as not stained with paint or blackberry juice. The garden contained our intimacy and sometimes our clashes of opinion, while outside stretched the sleepiest of Sussex cornfields, hemmed in only by the noble curve of Firle Beacon. In those days the passionate cooing of the wood pigeons or the plaintive mooing of cows were the most insistent among the noises off.

All this, it seemed, was not only controlled but had been created by Vanessa, in the same spirit attributed to God when He created the world. She had stretched out her hand and lo, Charleston, the Downs, the Weald and the watermeadows, even to a certain extent Lewes and Rodmell, Leonard and Virginia, came into existence full and complete and, during my childhood, unchanging. When, eventually, changes did occur, they were felt as a derogatory, underhand chipping away at a vision that had, in its day, however old fashioned or inconvenient, been near perfect. Vanessa, from her place at the diningroom table, carving the joint or pouring out coffee was demonstrably our only necessity. Life without her was inconceivable and when she did, very occasionally, absent herself, I immediately developed mumps or cut my finger on a new penknife, or some unexpected guest arrived who, with the best will in the world, turned everything topsy turvy.

Vanessa had another, equally significant place however, and that was at her easel, from where her gaze, although benign, was nevertheless concentrated in all its abstract remoteness on ravishing combinations of colour, light and shade, with which she seemed to carry on a constant communion. Separated from but aware of the habitual noises and rhythms of life in the background, she never lost touch with the Ariadne-like thread which connected her careful hand and large grey eye to the subject. Neither did she forget the demands of family life. When some inner sense of time, or the coolness of the evening forced itself on her consciousness, she would scrape her palette, tie her dirty brushes in a rag and take her box and canvas indoors, sighing with a mixture of pleasure and frustration.

It was time for pure joy to come to an end, but she was never idle. This was my hour, longed for and, I'm happy to say appreciated, not only by me but occasionally even by Clive and Duncan, when the latter did not continue to paint even after it was too dark to see. The gardenroom fire was lit and she read aloud from the Brontës, George Eliot or, more universally appreciated, from Jane Austen. Vanessa's voice was low, cool and controlled, lending a certain dignity even to the monologues of Miss Bates or the inanities of Mrs Bennet, coming into its own with the quiet if intolerable authority of Mr Knightley, and able mysteriously to suggest the final passionate concern of Mr Darcy for the distressed Elizabeth. Her greatest triumph was perhaps when I burst into tears on the death of George Osborne on the field of Waterloo . . . that was not at Charleston but, of all places, in a hotel not far from the Cobbe at Lyme Regis. I was jealous of my friend Eve, Mrs Younger's daughter, who had read *Persuasion* when I had not, and could therefore talk as an adult to Vanessa on a subject from which I was utterly excluded. But in truth Vanessa was not so much a dramatic as a tireless reader, soothing and almost hypnotic to listen to, and whose voice connects me as surely to the nineteenth century as though I had lived in it myself.

VI

Voyages

With my own parents, Vanessa Bell and Duncan Grant, I often went on voyages, from which however we always returned. If they were journeys out and away from English life, they were recognised as temporary escapes into a wider, more cosmopolitan world where the landmarks were nonetheless familiar links with both past and present, not only Raphael and Piero, but Matisse and Picasso. When we put up our easels, it was often in the vicinity of a Roman column or a building by Alberti, or in a landscape recalling Corot or Cézanne: we were infused by a feeling of continuity, a sort of spiritual kinship which, to my parents at least, was a source of pleasure and inspiration.

Vanessa would have preferred to travel invisibly, or at least incognito, enclosed within the bubble of her own dreams and abstractions, but she also took it for granted – as indeed did we – that it was her business to make all practical arrangements for our journey. It was she who went to the Wayfarer's Travel Agency, booked the tickets, did all the telephoning, had the car repaired, and left instructions for forwarding letters: she in fact who, while ensuring our safe return, took responsibility for the success or failure of our adventure.

For this is what we called it although, blessedly enough, no disasters ever happened. The excitement we felt at seeing the cliffs of Dover recede while those of Calais or Dieppe grew larger, was much like that of watching the lifting of the curtain at the theatre; but it was a curtain behind which we could actually penetrate, mixing with actors who were unconscious of the footlights, but played their rôle to perfection. English failings, too well known and understood, were temporarily suspended to allow the renewed enjoyment of half forgotten but newly appreciated habits and ways of living. Such things as good coffee, good food and general kindness oiled the wheels, and we counted them as luxuries. They were, more or less, the only ones: although Vanessa sometimes drove her own car, by the time it was packed it was so full that space for humans was limited and uncomfortable. Hotels were chosen for their ambiance rather than for comfort: in French ones the plumbing was deficient and the electricity dim, while in Italy both were deplorable and, before the Americans had won the war against parasites, there were often bed bugs and fleas to contend with. The only thing that was nearly always good was the food – prepared with more care than now. But all these things were peripheral – enjoyed if possible, laughed at or forgotten if not. The real purpose of the excursion was a state of mind, a communion with things seen, impossible to put into words, and yet, by small interjections, sighs and signs, shared. The tempo was slow and the temperature never high, but little was missed and a lot enjoyed.

Wherever we were, daily life followed much the same pattern as at home: breakfast, with as much hot coffee as could be commanded or procured, then a pause for a cigarette and the settling of accounts, and making a plan for the day. Then the disappearance of one and all to wash, collect brushes that had been carefully cleaned the evening before and left standing in the bathroom tooth mug, together with paint boxes, canvas or board, easel and so forth. Then to the motif, usually on foot, Vanessa's appearance reminiscent of the White Queen, Duncan's a mixture of Charlie Chaplin and an apache from the purlieus of Montmartre. He would of course help her with her paraphernalia, but if he chose to go in a different direction, it was then we might expect him to return accompanied by a new friend who was helping him with his own accoutrement. He had an extraordinary ability to concentrate on his canvas, while adding delicately little dabs of paint, and carrying on an over-simplified conversation in a foreign language, with some terribly serious and shy adolescent who fancied he too might become an artist. It may have been the strangely remote look in Duncan's eye, fastened not only on the subject but on his own vision of it, that attracted people. It was the same magnetism that operates between humans and certain animals which, while superficially friendly, proves to be incorruptibly aloof.

In Italy in particular both painters inevitably drew small crowds to watch their performance. There may be those whose temperament allows them to put on an act of painting, but neither Vanessa nor Duncan were capable of it. Vanessa would avoid such a situation whenever possible, even at the sacrifice of a more exciting view of her subject: she would choose the shadowy corner under a bridge or some ledge too small to accommodate anyone but herself.

But this wasn't always possible, and there were days when she would return for lunch exasperated by the antics of small urchins who hadn't been able to resist the temptation of putting their fingers into her delicious whorls of vermilion or cobalt and smearing it on their cheeks and noses. And in Rome, her totally unjustifiable faith in human nature led her to leave our passports on a nearby stone while concentrating on the cypresses in the Medici gardens – with foreseeable results which led to hours of questioning by the Fascist authorities.

Many evenings were spent writing letters about such hap-

65

penings, magnifying their importance to those at home to provoke laughter, which we at our café table would vicariously imagine, thus enjoying it twice over. After supper, when the lamps
were lit and the fountains playing, we would return to our iron
bedsteads and lumpy mattresses to sleep soundly, and start all
over again the following morning.

VII

The French Connection – Part 1

My life has been loosely, but pervasively, mixed up with France for as long as I can remember, and I can go so far as to say that nothing in it would be the same or have the same flavour, without this connection.

I was often told by Vanessa, to flatter and stimulate my interest, that I had French blood in my veins. Admittedly, since it dated from the eighteenth century, it had become pretty mixed with other sorts, but there was enough of it to be a source of pride: it gave us an excuse for linking our lives vicariously with the much admired nationality on the other side of the Channel.

By a sort of heroic disregard, Vanessa managed to avoid most aspects of snobbery: but I think there was some feeling of this sort in her attitude to the French. Like being in love, snobbery is a surrender to a powerful attraction for reasons beyond our control, and perhaps this mysterious condition appeared to be justified, in moments of uncertainty, by the knowledge that a great-great-grandmother had been married to a page of Marie Antoinette. But there were other inducements, of an infinitely more powerful nature, aroused by such painters as Corot, Chardin, Seurat and Cézanne, whose radiant and yet mercifully *terre-à-terre* solidity appealed to Vanessa hungering for the visual, as opposed to the literary experience.

It was in 1927, when I was nine, that Duncan, staying with his mother Ethel and her sister Daisy MacNeil at Cassis-sur-Mer, fell ill with suspected typhoid. Desperately anxious, and with me also on her hands, Vanessa decided to go there, taking both me, and our *bonne-à-tout-faire*, Grace Germany.

Cassis, 30 or more klms from Marseilles, was – or rather is – a small port and fishing village, beloved of painters because of its provincialism, its vineyards (which date from Roman times) and the incredible amount of sun which has the power to lull most anxieties. Aunt Daisy was the proud possessor of a yacht which she sometimes kept in the port, and it was this, probably, which led to her and Mrs Grant taking the Mimosa, a villa owned by Roland Penrose, situated just outside the town, hung over and honoured by the prominent and noble Couronne de Charlemagne.

We spent the first week or two of our stay in the Hotel Cendrillon, a step or two away from the port and within a stone's throw of the stinking beach, where little boys fished for sardines and lovers embraced in the sparse shadow of the rocks. Every day Vanessa would go to the Villa Mimosa, where a scruffy look-ing Duncan was slowly recovering, leaving me with Grace to learn French in the stuffy little salon of Mlle Chevalier, ex-schoolmistress and relic of what was loosely alluded to as the Ancien Régime. Honoured and respected by all, Mlle Chevalier was infinitely respectable, conservative and conventional, living with her old mother in the centre of the town. After going through a verb or two, we spent our mornings playing cards or snakes and ladders, stifling our yawns and wilting in the heat which pen-etrated the over-furnished room in spite of closed shutters and lace curtains. Eventually the sacred hour of Midi arrived and we would retire to the Hotel to eat a kind of food I took an instant dislike to, to lie afterwards on our beds in an unwilling surrender to the southern style of life.

Eventually Vanessa rented a little red and white box called the Villa Corsica, newly constructed and placed, as I remember, almost opposite the Villa Mimosa. But whereas the latter modestly recalled the *fin-de-siècle*, and had a wisteria and a mimosa in the garden, the Corsica, built as a speculation by the Doctor Agostini, rose out of a pile of dusty rubble, inhabited by large black ants. I remember our stay there as something of an ordeal punctuated by afternoon walks with a Grace pursued by a certain M. Grigorescu, one of the local artists, who 'popped up' as Grace said, out of hidden hollows and from behind stone walls, to ask her hand in marriage.

Exactly why Vanessa fell in love with Cassis enough to repair and rent Colonel Teed's La Bergére (which was not a Villa), I can only now surmise, since at the time we took it all so much for granted and knew no other part of France with which to compare it. Vanessa never bathed in the sea; but of course the Mediterranean had its uses as a line of blue or purple painted on a canvas. Neither did she care for the heat of summer, or for the kind of society that collected in the town. However, she didn't go to Cassis in the height of summer, and was not often there when the influx of visitors was at its greatest. What she did like was the dazzling purity of the light, the mixture of blue, ochre and silver in the landscape, accentuated by the black trunks of vine and olive. And always at Cassis she was on holiday, the English responsibilities were lifted off her shoulders. At La Bergère she was relaxed, soothed by the presence of the beautiful and dignified Elise, who cooked us food fresh from the market on a bed of charcoal incorporated into the kitchen stove. The chore of fetching her from the crowded little back street in which she lived was shared by Duncan or Peter Teed, and made in any case a delicious change from England, rumbling in our old car down the lane bordered by wild tulips and anemones, under branches of almond or cherry blossom. Elise took Grace under

69

her wing and taught her how to cook with herbs and olive oil.

For Vanessa, if not for Duncan, seclusion was a prime necessity, and La Bergère was as well placed as Charleston for being out of it. Although we were so conscious of its not being England, it was not really France either. Under a fiercer sky and in a hotter climate, it was Charleston reconstituted, albeit on a smaller scale. For one season I was blessed with a French Governess called Sabine, but I never went to a French school and had no French friends of my own age: neither were we called on by the local French families – it would have been extraordinary if it had been otherwise. Our acquaintances were either wandering painters of various nationalities, or expatriate colonels and their wives. They all led very agreeable lives, lounging in cafés, basking in the sun either in their gardens or at their easels, and drinking the local wine.

At the deepest level Cassis was, for Vanessa, simply another light by which to see things. Being what she was, motivated on the one hand by her love of painting and on the other by her love of Duncan, she took from France what suited her best, and left the rest to look after itself. Quite uninterested in the higher echelons of social life, not in the least sharing Clive's desire to take part in brilliant and witty conversation in the Proustian salons of Princesses and Ambassadors, Vanessa's sympathy and humour were aroused more pertinently by her daily practical relationships with odd-job men, garagistes and *bonnes-à-tout-faire*, for whom she often felt admiration and affection, and who seemed to her refreshingly full of dignity and common-sense.

She was relieved too to find, in all walks of life, such an ingrained professionalism – an echo of that important French word *'serieux'* which seemed to her lacking in England. It permeated not only the world of the businessman and the winegrower, but also that of the artist. In France, as perhaps in all Latin countries, being a painter was a matter of joy and self-congratulation as well as a purely practical profession, full of enthralling questions on the subject of what the Bussys called 'cadmium': talk about oil and turpentine, brushes, paint and canvas. All this was immensely refreshing for Vanessa, whose sense of insecurity suffered in England from a mixture of patronising incomprehension or complete indifference. It was not of course that these did not exist in France – but the artists put up a better defence against them.

Cassis – or was it Vanessa and her easy-going, generous way of life – also attracted all our friends who, as La Bergère was too small, put up either with Peter and Jean Teed at the nearby Château de Fontcreuse, or somewhere in the town. This made hospitality merely a matter of food and drink, and the ability to give the impression that you had all the time in the world to spend in the most delightful art of all – conversation. That this was a French art *par excellence* was of course recognised, and although this had suffered a sea change in crossing the Channel, one could say that it was indulged in as a conscious tribute to French brilliance. But brilliance was not what Vanessa liked best. She preferred the sense of reality she found when listening to such artists as Segonzac or Derain or, in later days, Pierre Clairin, talking of things they knew *à fond*, through personal experience rather than theory.

Considering how much she hungered for this attitude it may seem strange that she was not on more intimate terms with either these or any other painters in France. She was, I am sure, much admired both as a personality and as an artist, but the warmth and hospitality of the French never seems to have extended beyond cafés and restaurants and, sometimes, studios. The relationship was a professional one, inhibited perhaps by a certain shyness and formality on Vanessa's side, and on theirs by a feeling that Vanessa and Duncan, as a couple, and foreigners at that, could not be integrated into their own family lives. For my part I regret that I never knew or was in a position to fraternise with their children.

For Vanessa, the opportunity to live if only for part of the year in France, was a way of feeling closer to French painting through the climate and landscape. Cassis was not far from l'Estaque and within easy reach of the Montagne Ste Victoire which had so often inspired Cézanne, while further along the coast, where the sky may have been a shade bluer, were places associated with Renoir, Bonnard and Matisse, all painters she admired.

Another painter lived there too, in the hills above Menton, and that was Simon Bussy, old friend of Matisse and mentor of Duncan's, married to Dorothy Strachey, Duncan's cousin. My parents held all three Bussys in the greatest esteem and affection, but for some obvious reasons and for others less so, we made no effort to meet each other on the coast of France. Travel was more difficult in those days and the Bussys had no car and, even more important, I suspect that both Vanessa and Simon clung to their paint pots and easels, suspicious of the invasive sociability that would have been the result of such an effort. A greater objection on Vanessa's part may have been that the Bussys were too intellectual, too high-brow. Dorothy Bussy, although one of the gentlest of women, and with a sweet though austere sense of humour, remained rigorously Strachey, approaching every question in a spirit of passionate discrimination which, I think, rather put the wind up Vanessa who may also have imagined, at the thought of going over to Roquebrune, that she would be asked to meet such distinguished and familiar friends of the Bussys as André Gide, Roger Martin-du-Gard or Paul Valéry.

As a family the Bussys were double edged, or double faced, never, as a whole, being completely at home, since they spent half the year in England and the other half in France. Janie, of mixed blood, was the most at ease – although different – in each place, but Dorothy, in spite of her encyclopaedic knowledge of French, remained Strachey to the core.

Simon Bussy however never became in the slightest degree English, maintaining a kind of bantam intransigence in spite of all the northerly winds that blew. I well remember, in the huge and rather gloomy Strachey drawing-room at 51 Gordon Square, on the occasion of the family's annual cocktail party, his sudden and passionate denial of the greatness of Rubens. Even Duncan was shocked, but it was, I think, a freak judgement due partly to age and, perhaps, to personal disappointment. For Simon Bussy, living most of his life almost next door to Matisse, and frequently appealed to by the great man for his opinion, had never known success on that scale. His was a *succès d'estime*, an appreciation felt by all those who had eyes to see the skill, the delicacy and the masterliness of his work: but perhaps the things he set most store by, while more original, appealed least. So he took refuge in taciturnity, stubbornness and strange opinions. But he was a great man – a small great man, whose inner life was a secret, who worked like a beaver in pursuit of an idea naturally unrealisable, but austere and powerful enough to tame the ego, which escaped in other ways. His quintessential, peasant-like Frenchness was keenly appreciated by both Vanessa and Duncan, who respected but did not dare contradict him: he was a man who knew his métier.

In their house at Roquebrune, I was Dorothy's guest more than Simon's. But Dorothy was something of a guest even in her own house. It was Simon who attended to the housekeeping. He may even have done the shopping but he certainly ordained what was to be bought and how it was to be cooked. Woe betide the *bonne* if, as after 60 years it is still printed on my memory, she put a little too much salt in the salad dressing! One felt that, even if there were other things she did wrong, she would hardly do that again, after the rebuke administered by Simon at the dinner table. I felt however that his *'sérieux'*, applied as fiercely to the finer points of gastronomy as it was to the selection of his pastels, was admirable.

Dorothy, who did not care so much about the salt, took his perfectionism for granted, regarding him, as he her, with profound and affectionate detachment. So separate did they often seem, although hardly ever seen apart, that one could easily imagine them, as in the 18th Century, calling each other Monsieur and Madame. It was a way of rubbing along beyond the confines of matrimony. They had learned to live with each other as friends and companions and were, in spite of their very different interests, at one in their sincerity. Dorothy's greatest love was literature, whereas Simon was a painter to the soles of his feet. It goes without saying however that both were cultured, each capable of looking beyond their own garden into that of the other with an appreciation that was both loving and, like the best of champagne, a little dry. Dorothy's letters to Gide reveal how much she understood Simon's nature and painting; and although it is likely that Simon neither knew Shakespeare by heart nor cared much for Jacobean poetry, he must have recognised and respected Dorothy's feelings – hardly short of adoration – for both these subjects.

In her sulphur yellow drawing room, Dorothy sat hunched, immensely quiet and concentrated, while the French windows, opening onto terraces of olives, oranges and lemon trees, disclosed the tips of blue irises and in the distance, the sea. She lived in the décor created by her husband, who was every bit as knowledgeable a gardener as he was a cook.

The French Connection – Part 2

In 1936 I had been sent to Paris, like so many English girls of my kind, to learn French, and my hosts were old friends of the Bussy's. Jean Vanden Eckhoudt, of Flemish origin, had been another student friend of Simon Bussy's, and had become yet one more painter enamoured of the South and its splendour. A remarkable artist, he was also a solitary one – a little too saint-like for ordinary purposes. He married a woman who gave up a career as a singer to be the artist's wife par excellence, practical, kind and full of common sense, and a mordant wit which sprang from the fact that she was not easily impressed by the pretentions and superficialness of other people. As a refugee in the first World War, offered asylum by Sir William Lancaster and his wife, she was astonished to see the amount of uneaten food left on people's plates, and horrified to learn that it was afterwards all thrown away! Knowing of the near starvation in Belgium this struck her forcibly, and was held ever after against the English as a sign of their barbarity. No one could say that she was altogether wrong!

It was after this experience that the Vandens, as they were known, came to live at La Couala, a tiny house up the hill from the Bussys at La Souco. They had a daughter, Zoum who, living so close, spent much of her childhood and youth with the Bussys. The grown-ups had thought it perfect for her to become a friend of Janie's. But Janie was a solitary, fragile child who preferred playing with her collection of hand-made, stuffed animals, and

75

Zoum, who was precociously mature as well as a little older, attached herself more to Dorothy Bussy, fast becoming not only pupil but friend. This explained the fact that she spoke English with more than an echo of the Strachey accent, and had read all the English novelists as well as a great deal of English poetry.

At La Couala Zoum grew up in the greatest simplicity, often dipping into the more intellectually sophisticated life that went on in the Strachey-Bussy ménage, where she met their friends including Gide who, at first impressed, became fond of her. Physically strong and splendid, there was a tinge of masculinity in her beauty which she knew how to exploit by wearing a black sombrero, and cutting her hair into two dark *favoris*, one in front of each ear. Had she smoked a cigar, she would have been the Carmen of her day. Very musical, and with a theatrical flair that later became transmuted into that of a marvellous raconteuse, she began life with the ambition of becoming a concert pianist. But one recital, given, I think, in Nice, was enough. Mysteriously lacking the confidence which in other situations seemed to exude from her, she turned to painting. When she was not helping her mother with a brother fourteen years younger than she was, whom she had helped bring into the world, she stood in front of her easel under a pine tree or in some pool of shade painting the shimmering walls of Roquebrune.

And then a young man appeared, as if from nowhere, although actually from Paris, convalescent from a breakdown or an unhappy attachment. He was a friend of friends of the Bussys, was extremely intelligent, handsome, bearded and Jewish, and his name was François Walter. Bowled over by the atmosphere of free, intellectual humanism which he discovered in the yellow drawing-room at La Souco, he was at first more attracted by the mysterious and brittle charm of Janie. But it was with Zoum that he fell deeply and forever in love: to which emotion she responded with some reserve, strongly attracted but not wishing to leave her parents or the passionate peace and equilibrium of her life in the south.

But they married, moved to an apartment in the district of Auteuil in Paris – in no way an artist's quarter – and became an attractive and interesting couple, struggling to live in a civilized way, and hoping for children. For Zoum was nothing if not maternal. If related to Carmen, she was also descended from those large ladies in velvet gowns and a hat with a feather, painted by LaTour. And at the same time she suggested a peasant woman in a picture by Millet, her hair half down, nursing a baby.

For something like eight years however she remained childless, and continued to paint large figure compositions with vaguely religious overtones in browns and ochres, using her parents as models. Occasionally she shook the dust of Paris from her feet and disappeared for a time to Roquebrune or to Gargilesse, where her landscapes became greener. François, earning their living at the Cour des Comptes, and becoming more and more aware of the threat of Hitler and war, committed himself to an ardent pacifism and ran a small newspaper called *Vigilance* . He also wrote poetry and some art criticism. I particularly remember – partly because it came as a surprise to me to know he wrote at all about painting – an excellent article on Seurat.

It was of course Janie who recommended them as just the right hosts for the young and unformed, such as me. They had already had a member of the Rendel-Strachey clan and as this had been a success, they accepted me too, only to find, with some dismay, that I was infinitely less independent, much more inclined to hang around Zoum in her studio, to play the piano and the violin within earshot, and to be in for most meals. But Zoum, generously understanding, took me under her wing, educated me and sympathised with me, and became a second mother to me. It was when at last she became pregnant that, feeling preoccupied and exhausted, she devised the plan of sending me to stay with first the Bussys and then her own parents.

I have described elsewhere something of my life with Zoum and François in Paris, and there is not time now to say much more. They were extraordinary, both proving to be an important addition to my life – but there were many other things as well: Paris itself for example, and the process of becoming familiar with it. I regret now not having been more systematic in my exploration of the city with the express purpose of getting to know it better, although after the war I partly made up for this lack of enterprise. But I do remember an afternoon in the *quartier* St Germain with Zoum and Clive on one of his periodical visits to Paris. A mixture of curiosity about Zoum and a desire to educate me led him to entertain us at La Pérouse – a far more unassuming and less expensive restaurant then than now – with Dunoyer de Segonzac. He was a painter and etcher, often making portraits of Colette, a neighbour of his at St Tropez, or line drawings of Isadora Duncan dancing. Quite likely that it was at La Pérouse that I ate my first oysters, but it was Segonzac's eyes, that resembled them, that I most clearly remember. He also was a *bon viveur,* combining with ease his taste for the worldly with his gifts as an artist. Well dressed in a pale grey suit for lunch with Zoum and my stepfather Clive, he talked with authority about life in general. He had the quality so envied by Vanessa of taking himself and his art seriously without affectation or pretension. After lunch he departed, and Clive, Zoum and I wandered along the narrow streets with our chins tilted upwards and our eyes directed by Clive to various architectural details and objects of beauty. I was delighted to find that Clive liked Zoum, who in turn remembered this afternoon through a haze of appreciation.

It was during the same winter that I was also invited by Clive to dine with André Derain and his wife Alice. They had a niece of my age and thought we might hit it off together. All that I remember of the house, which was, I think, in Neuilly, is the dining-room, mostly because, as in most French houses, we sat long over the meal – which consisted of eels stewed in white wine – rather than, as in England, moving into some other room. There was an impressive hunting horn hanging on the wall, which Derain removed and on which he blew a note as powerful as his person and presence, to please me! Flattering. I was raring to go on all levels, but his niece was, although charming, shy and timid – probably much better brought up: wouldn't play piano duets. Alice Derain, who had cooked the meal, was quiet and motherly: she had the allure of the traditional artist's wife. The atmosphere was domestic but lively, and at that moment I would have said there was not so much difference as all that between Derain's *foyer* and that of Charleston.

In order to appreciate the intensity with which Clive strove to assimilate and sometimes imitate French manners and habits, one has to remember how English – one might say how primevally English – his own background was and, conversely, the impact that Paris and French life and art must have had on a young man accustomed to fox hunting and grouse shooting, and the subtle but inhibited joys of a writer such as Jane Austen – an author all the Bell family knew by heart. No wonder that the art of Toulouse Lautrec and Degas, the *cafés chantants* and the *bars zincs*, the cynicism, vitality and elegance of Paris went, if not to his head, then to support his longing to escape from Ye Olde England, and particularly his father.

For Clive (as for so many others) the most civilized people in the world were the French, whose priorities as regards the arts were so different from those of the English. No doubt he knew a lot about painting, his chosen subject: but I always felt that he was more at ease with the written word, more intimately inspired by the vision of life called up for example by Proust, and a desire to relive and perpetuate it, simply because he could not bear it to disappear and leave him in the cold.

Clive was gifted for being an observer, for living vicariously. But he was also an educator, someone whose vision consisted of mutual communication and exchange. It was a vision he wanted to share and happily had enough money to do so. He was a great reader with exceptional memory and a keen sense of history, and wanted to make me aware that living one's own life is not enough: one is also living history and cannot separate one's own life from the past.

It was to him that I owe the opening of the myriad doors of French Literature. In taking it for granted that I could read French, Clive actually aroused me to the effort of doing so. I plunged into Mérimée (a great favourite of his), Candide, Maupassant and *Les Liaisons Dangereuses*, the latter proposed, I'm convinced, in an effort to awaken my sexuality. I was indeed thrilled by it but my reaction had little to do with sex: far more with the superb language, which I read without really understanding. It was perhaps a shocking book, but I was too accustomed to theoretical immorality for it to have a liberating effect.

Clive learnt French, he told me, in the opposite way from me, by looking up every word he did not understand in the dictionary: and in a short while he knew the language fairly well. He went on learning of course – I could depend on him for the accurate translation of difficult passages. He would have given anything to speak French like a native, and was only prevented from doing so by his damned Englishness which somehow got in the way. The idiomatic phrases which he knew so well didn't trip off his tongue with quite the sound he would have liked. And yet he continued to repeat them, hoping to prove his love and admiration for the most remarkable people in the world.

It was easy to laugh at Clive for his snobbery which, though unavowed, was transparent. But it wasn't quite so simple. True, he was, like most men of the world, both class and career conscious: but he respected the distinguished and the great for qualities he was too modest to claim for himself, and needed or longed to fête them, to celebrate their distinction. In doing so he affirmed his own participation, playing the role of *entremetteur* and even impresario. Incapable of showing his emotions, which were probably as deep as anyone's, there was always a schism between his heart and his intelligence, which provided a smoke screen to shield his sensibilities. What remained however was an inextinguishable curiosity about life or lives that were being transformed under his eyes into history which for him had such powerful charms. It was this feeling that he tried to convey to others, that animated his dinner and lunch parties, his sorties across the Channel, his accounts of ravishing, intimate soirées with Marie-Louise Bosquet or Bousquet, who knew all the strands of malicious gossip that went round Paris. If, at Charleston, Vanessa was frankly bored, and the rest of us laughed up our sleeves, Duncan was, or pretended to be, intrigued and responded to Clive with a more civilized feeling than the rest of us.

I cannot of course speak on this subject without mentioning Roger Fry, since it was he who did most, beyond the confines of social life, to make French and English artists aware of each other. But I was too young when he died to have any experience of France in his company. I can only say that for him French life and culture were of incalculable importance, leading him to lead a life so deeply and humanely civilized that Clive could only goggle and, with some laughter, approve, although Roger's conception of civilization was in many ways so far removed from his own.

It was through Roger that we came to know the remarkable Maurons who were of great importance for Julian. They were, I suppose, more essentially French than anyone else we knew, born and brought up in St-Rémy-de-Provence, speaking Provençal far more readily than English. Charles's father had been Mayor of St-Rémy, an office that Charles himself was later to hold. He was rooted in the Latin-Mediterranean tradition, symbolised by the fact that he lived almost next door to the ancient Greek town of Glanum, situated close to the group of Roman buildings known as Les Antiquités. A broad, solid southerner, Charles was typical of a civilization which produces peasants who, while cultivating their patch of vines, are also intellectuals. In his case the intellectual dominated, particularly as, with very poor sight, he could hardly see to cut the grapes. He eventually became a Professor at Aix University where a chair was expressly created for him to expound his newly conceived literary criticism based on psychological interpretation – very fascinating and fairly abstruse. His wife Marie, full of vivacity and warmth, was a schoolmistress and became an author, writing high comedy about her native country. They kept open house, particularly it would seem for Julian and some of his Cambridge friends, providing them with a particularly generous form of rigorous discussion – a style of questioning which, of course, could also be found in Cambridge or Bloomsbury, but was perhaps in France more critical and realistic. Although older than Julian the Maurons were still young, and cared deeply about politics and the state of the world. This of course was getting worse, and finally led to Julian's death in the Spanish Civil War. So that Vanessa, for whom the Maurons were a shade too literary, got to know a different side of them in her search for sympathy and help after that event, when in 1938 we drove over from Cassis to see them in their Mas on the outskirts of St-Rémy.

For me Charles was a father figure, gentle, smiling and very attractive if, partly no doubt due to language problems, a little unapproachable. Marie took charge, bustling, hospitable and kind, full of shrewd laughter. After lunch, which I am sure consisted of *daube*, the rest of us faded out to allow a sad Vanessa to talk to a sensitive and considerate Charles about her son. It was a visit, memorable enough, of which I wish I could remember more, but from which I culled impressions which went deep. Later, the Maurons came to England and to Charleston and, long after their separation and Charles' death, I went again to the Mas, and saw an elderly Marie, dancing in triumph in celebration of François Mitterand as President.

The French Connection – Part 3

Vanessa still clung to Cassis. In 1938 she, Duncan, Quentin and I drove there, going down the west side of France, through Thury-Harcourt, where we ate an omelette stuffed with onions, tomatoes, herbs and garlic, ladled over with cream and a powdering of cheese and briefly browned under the grill. I cannot now find the recipe in *Larousse Gastronomique* (the same copy that we had at Charleston in those days) and have forgotten its name: but I still make it on occasion. Much of our French culture began with gastronomic experience: even the smallest and least expensive restaurant, discovered in a little town hardly larger than the Cliffe in Lewes, would provide one with a copious and *sérieux* meal, and Quentin and I would plan our day in relation to the *spécialités* that we hoped to sample. Thus, after going through Angoulème and Perigueux, where we ate stuffed neck of goose and possibly *paté de fois gras*, depending on whether, at that period of his life, Duncan had rejected it on grounds of cruelty to the goose, we stopped at Castelnaudary to eat the famous Cassoulet – which, I seem to remember, none of us liked.

Vanessa, always frugal in her eating, must have found all this rather irrelevant and juvenile; but she tolerated it, relieved, I imagine, to see her children enjoying themselves. Duncan gazed at the landscape and smiled hazily, while Quentin proved a catalyst who, while satisfying my youthful curiosity, bought and read newspapers, recounting to us the progress of the Munich crisis as it rumbled threateningly across Europe. Lists of those to be called up were posted on the doors of the local Mairies, and glum groups of men gathered in the cafés. I detected a spirit of fatalism so far removed from my own longing to live life to the full that, once Quentin had returned to La Bergère waving a copy of *The Times* with a photograph of Vanessa's old acquaintance Neville Chamberlain and his umbrella, returning in a kind of shabby triumph from Munich, I again buried my head in the sand . . .

Cassis accepted us again, after an interval of perhaps two or three years. Vanessa was acutely conscious of the passage of time, revealed by this return to old haunts where she had been so happy. As of old Elise came to do the cooking and renewed her intimacy with Vanessa, while Duncan painted and I fell in love with a very attractive English officer on board a battleship anchored in Marseilles. When we eventually said goodbye to Jean and Peter Teed, even I realised that time was running out. And, only a year later, we were completely cut off. Very soon silence prevailed. All our friends, the Bussys, the Walters, the Teeds, and various artists, the Maurons and many others became incommunicado, although Janie managed from time to time to smuggle a letter out. Our imagination was hard put to it to realise anything like the truth of their experience, and it was inevitable, perhaps, that we should either exaggerate, or minimalise its dangers. We had after all our own traumatic experiences to live through, which included Virginia's suicide, at once a personal tragedy and a symbol of the fragility of the values we had hitherto lived by.

But France and its culture became even more necessary. Submerged although it seemed to be, and partly because of this, it exercised a powerful, if unattainable fascination, and it was now, rather than when I was living with the Walters, that I made a conscious effort to learn the language. Living in James and Alix Strachey's house in Gordon Square, I talked to myself in French as I did the housework, becoming conversant with ordinary, every day expressions to suit most occasions. After much solitary practice, they later proved extremely useful; and even led me to offer help one day to some French officers in the Euston Road, who did not know which bus to take. This earned me thanks and a salute of great politesse.

My husband David Garnett, or Bunny, worked in Bush House sending messages and propaganda to those trapped in France, and we occasionally entertained parachutists who were dropped to help the Resistance. Although they could not talk freely, some idea seeped through to me of the conditions that prevailed. Towards the end of the war François who, because of his Jewish blood and political opinions had been on the run, arrived in London. He got himself a job in the Treasury and lived with us till Zoum came, in a state of suicidal exhaustion, with her young daughter Sylvie. And then the Bussys appeared, much as if they were still pursuing their pre-war peregrination, but underfed and without clothes, to find rationing in full force and no compensatory black market on our austere and puritanical shores. Janie too had risked her life in working for the Resistance, but remained silent on the subject. The Teeds had been banished by the Germans to the mountains further north, but had not, I think, suffered much. Peter died but Jean survived and came to visit us at Hilton, where I lived after my marriage to Bunny.

Although I thought of France as having been victimised, I never thought of her as defeated. Although things were inevitably and perhaps disastrously changed, it was also extraordinary how the innate conservatism of the French – so deplored by François – maintained its grip on provincial life and how, in the towns and villages, one was more aware of a life-style closer to that of Flaubert and Balzac than of that of the English or Americans.

I well remember the emotions of stepping ashore at Dieppe

for the first time after the war with Vanessa and Duncan, and how we were assailed by the sudden rush of French resilience and vitality mixed with the cries of the ever present seagulls cruising overhead in their aggressive and competitive search for a living. Vanessa always took a drug called Somnifene for the ordeal of the crossing, arriving on the other side of the Channel in a hazy and sleepy state of mind which was supposed to wear off quite fast. But I sometimes wondered whether it didn't colour her whole view of France, enabling her to enjoy the general feeling of *dépaysement* and irresponsibility, entering a country which was so delightfully familiar and yet not her own. In their variably faded blue trousers, even the porters seemed more likely to think of painting as a serious profession rather than something that, as a woman, one dabbled in for lack of something better to do. But on the rest of the journey to Paris on the SNCF, for which there was often time for an excellent lunch in the restaurant car, put her *d'applomb*, ready for a delicious initiatory evening in Paris doing nothing but sniff the air and register the unbelievable difference between it and London.

The small, unpretentious Hôtel de Londres in the rue Bonaparte, with a red plush staircarpet and stuffy bedrooms straight out of Vuillard had become, over the years, a familiar refuge from which to saunter out, as a preliminary tonic, to the Louvre just over the Pont des Arts, with its Ingres, Chardins and Veroneses. Vanessa and Duncan visited all the significant exhibitions, which then offered havens of peace and quiet in which to examine work either new or loved for its familiarity which, however, always presented some new aspect. Outside these spacious temples of culture buzzed the lively, irresistible city in which there was always time to enjoy a leisurely meal in some favourite restaurant.

And there was always the café, usually Les Deux Magots, where one could sip coffee, wait for friends, and consider what to do next. Hours were spent there, looking, watching, and often secretly sketching under the table, so as neither to offend nor provoke unwanted interest. Tiny sketch books were filled with rapid portraits in thick black pencil, of heads and bodies, expressing Vanessa's wonder at the variety yet sameness of humanity, and the humour with which she regarded it.

Vanessa absorbed sights in much the same way that other people absorb sounds, without immediate speculation as to why they interested her. It would be difficult to exaggerate the extent to which she lived through her eyes and, concomitantly, through her visual memory. A continuous tapestry of painting seemed to unroll itself at the back of her mind, sparking off analogies with the immediate sights which surrounded her. In desultory café conversation she might point out to Duncan a lady wearing a scarf which reminded her of a particular blue in a portrait by Ingres or David, and this would lead to a discussion of blue and the emotions aroused by it, ending inevitably by saying how French it was – a blue unattainable in England since the days of Gainsborough!

Nevertheless, it was not through history or literature that Vanessa saw the French. Unlike Clive, she did not wish to identify with them or to prove how well she knew them. She spoke French with an unmistakable accent – not quite the usual one, having been taught by a series of French governesses – but she was too self-conscious and shy to want to shine in this way, and was entirely without social ambitions. Her demands were impossible: she wanted to communicate with the chosen, ineffably intelligent and sensitive people she felt French artists to be, and yet she preferred to remain alone to look about her, and to remember afterwards what had amused her. Her distinction, beauty and seriousness impressed the French: when she did consent to say something, it must have been clear that she knew what she was talking about. But her inherent reserve created a barrier in addition to the one of culture and language: the only couple we became in the least intimate with was Line and Pierre Clairin.

I do not know how they entered Duncan's and Vanessa's lives, and cannot clearly remember when it was that I felt myself included in the friendship, but think that it was not until after 1945. Pierre was another father figure, to whom I gravitated because of his enthusiasm and vitality. He seemed to have perfected the art of communication, and was both passionate and boyish, wise and disarmingly innocent. Perfectly equal to the ways of the world, he was never taken in by them, and was happiest in his studio or his garden, or shopping for cheese – the best of its kind – in his local town. Culturally French, full of discernment and savoir faire, it came as a surprise to learn that he had an American mother and, sandwiched in somewhere, Jewish blood. Although he was a painter who embarked readily on large canvasses, he was at his best in small and delicate colour lithographs, many of which can be seen on the walls of Charleston. The blocks were usually cut by his wife Line, and were for him a mere offshoot, sent to his friends at Christmas time.

By nature as well as profession he was a teacher, and must I think have been one of the best as well as the most popular since he had an extraordinary gift for communicating his pleasure in the numerous techniques of printing, about which he knew all there was to know. A certain aura accrued to him in Vanessa's and Duncan's eyes because he had been a pupil of Sérusier, who had, in turn, been a friend of Gauguin. And because we usually saw him on his own ground – and in France all ground became his as soon as he trod on it – Vanessa and Duncan deferred to him as though he were senior to them, whereas in fact he must have been several years younger. And he frequently had, as many father figures do, his moments of boyish glee and innocence, when his face would uncrumple into a smile of infectious gaiety and Line would glance at him with an expression of very slightly ironic understanding.

Line devoted every fibre of her being to her husband without losing an iota of her very strong, but retiring, personality. Pierre was the active partner, the chooser and decider, but although she carried out his wishes, she never relinquished her own judgement or freedom of thought, and when it came, as it quite often did, to painter's gossip she showed a certain dry capacity to enjoy other people's weaknesses. But it was Pierre who did the talking, without however forgetting Line's presence. One could hardly imagine one without the other, and when indeed, after Duncan's death, Line died, Pierre followed her within a year.

Pierre knew everything that was going on in Paris, as well as all the painters of his generation and older, such as Derain, Marchand and Segonzac – indeed it was quite possibly through this last, who saw in Vanessa both goddess and artist successfully united, that she and my father had made Pierre's acquaintance. At all events, every time they found themselves in Paris he invited them to a meal either at Brasserie Lipp, or in some other well chosen restaurant that was a favourite of the moment.

As host he was perfect, paying great attention to all the preliminaries of the meal. Food and wine were important, but conversation infinitely more so. He could hardly wait to start talking and, although he didn't show it, may have found Vanessa and Duncan a shade too passive. They waited for him to start the ball rolling about the Parisian art world, of the shadier side of which they were only dimly aware but longed to know more. And Pierre's gossip was not entirely without an honest malice, relished also by Line. But it did not last long: seeing Vanesssa'a and Duncan's perfect innocence and English detachment, Pierre would switch to art itself, to Cézanne, exhibitions, or to types of ink or – that miracle – the Maroger medium.

Of these things he talked with masterly authority, a knowledge of detail, a conviction of their importance entirely lacking in my parents. They were interested certainly – but only with the tips of their whiskers, and had the maddeningly superior smile of those who have privately decided not to become involved. For them no canvas, paper, brushes or makes of colour seemed all that important: if necessary they could do without or find a substitute. Above all they could laugh at their predicament and get on with painting. Even if the results were unexpected they could if necessary be brushed on one side or taken advantage of.

But for Pierre such an attitude was unthinkable. He knew not only what he wanted, but what was necessary: nothing else would do, and Paris must be scoured to find it. In those days Paris could usually provide it, and Pierre knew exactly where to go: just as he knew where to get the best cheese and coffee. But some things could only be found in London, and once I was asked to comb likely shops for steel pen nibs of a special shape that could no longer be found in France. He detested a ball point or felt nib: these had just come on the market and absolutely thrilled Vanessa and Duncan, who bought them by the dozen and handed them round to all the family, fascinated by their total lack of sensitivity – the very fact that so disgusted Pierre. His insistence on the 'best', his tireless discrimination and satisfaction in finding the 'right' thing, his pleasure in the rapidly disappearing French *artisanat*, amused and charmed Vanessa and Duncan, but in its intense professionalism had the effect of making them feel out of it, even slightly unreal.

Were they insensitive, or just lazy? Were they simply amateurs, or was Pierre more of an epicurean than an artist? These questions hovered, and were unanswerable. But although Pierre was something of an epicurean, he was much more than that. A brief biography reveals an extraordinary life: in the first war he had been a flying ace, and could tell amazing stories of his exploits and escapes – one plane apparently made of balsa wood and canvas torn to ribbons first by German bullets and then by landing inopportunely in a tree, or on a sheet of water mistaken for a road, his gunner dead but he himself always miraculously untouched. He said that he never felt a moment's fear. . . ! Then there was marriage, children – in connection with whom there was some seldom mentioned tragedy – and Line, his second wife, in addition to his career as a *peintre-graveur*, teacher at the Beaux Arts and his resistance in the second war, culminating in his becoming an Academician. I was present on the occasion of his inauguration, when Pierre read an extraordinarily well written appreciation of Darius Milhaud, whom he was replacing, in front of his colleagues dressed, as he was himself, in breeches and coats embroidered with oak leaves in green and gold silk. In addition to all this he was an expert gardener and a passionate lover of late romantic music such as early Schönberg, to which he introduced me. After Duncan's death I stayed for a week with Pierre at St Loup where life was a sort of divine apology for Heaven, and where for a brief and concentrated moment I began to feel a real intimacy with this enchanting man.

There is no time to say more, and I have probably said too much already without getting anywhere near the heart of the matter. I have left out much that was important: Nan and Ethel Sands at Auppegard, Duncan's reactions and pleasures, Michel Saint-Denis and my own present life in the South. But perhaps I have said enough to show how necessary France and the French were to us all.

VIII

A Propos of the Simon Bussy Exhibition at Beauvais

This was written for *The Charleston Magazine* as an attempt to convey my pleasure in the exhibition of Simon Bussy's work in the Museum at Beauvais, to which I had lent four pastels bought at Sotheby's soon after Simon's death. After my own death three of them will go to the Museum.

Simon Bussy is little known to the general public, since most of his work is in private collections and this exhibition is, I think, the only one man show to have taken place since his death in 1954. Born in 1870, pupil of Gustave Moreau and friend and contemporary of Matisse, much admired by André Gide, Simon exhibited during his lifetime in both Paris and London, but never had more than a modest success. It may be that his work, refined and delicate as it is, was too reminiscent of the old masters and insufficiently avant-garde for the first half of the twentieth century. Or it may have something to do with the fact that he married into the intensely literary Strachey family, dividing his time between France and England, that denied him the appreciation he might have aroused had he stayed in the same country.

Judging from the distinction of the guests and the prevailing feeling of warmth at the Private View, the exhibition is, as I write, destined to be a huge success. For those who knew little or nothing of Simon, and they were the larger part, it was a delightful revelation, while for those who were aware of his work, it was a just, if tardy, celebration.

Modestly, even Mlle Marie-José Salmon, Directrice of the Museum who has organised the show so superbly, said that previously she had scarcely known who Simon was. But this, it seems to me, was the natural consequence of Simon's own attitude to himself, his life and his work, common to many artists at the beginning of the century, who considered it immoral to look for publicity as such. If fame sought out the artist, as for example with Simon's old friend and fellow artist Matisse, it was because he was one of the great. But had Simon sought to advertise himself, even on a modest scale, it would have been both vulgar and irrelevant.

Such a genuinely austere point of view was common to both Simon and his wife Dorothy and it gave them, in the eyes of others, if not in their own, an extraordinary strength of purpose and apparent sense of security. It was said, in my family, that Simon suffered because, although highly respected, he had never enjoyed a success comparable with that of Matisse, and that it was this which made him rather farouche and difficult. There may or may not have been some truth in such an analysis, but if so the pain was never enough to perturb Simon's conception of life and behaviour, which set true pride alongside a certain modesty, and a constant struggle for self knowledge against an appreciation of the dangers of excessive popularity.

One of the results of this rigorously moral outlook may have been his otherwise rather surprising changes of style and subject. Like a yacht tacking in a contrary wind, he veered from the modest and sobre pastels and oils of early years, which connect him

to the mainstream of the European tradition, to the more fashionable pictures of elegant and attractive ladies seen in the ambiance of the Promenade des Anglais, or his own villa *La Souco*,
painted in thick and sensuous impasto.

For me these are fascinating less for their artistic merit than
for their psychological unexpectedness in the work of an artist
whose most moving visions are of the inner life of his subject,
human or animal. In spite of their splendour there is in these
pictures a certain artificiality which does not seem characteristic.
And yet, in all Simon's work, there is a strong desire for formality, for finding the design which will best express his sense of the
spiritual aspect of his subject.

It was natural, in the twenties and thirties, to find inspiration
in the formal contrivances of Art Nouveau, and it may be imper-
tinent to regret the desire of the artist to exploit its possibilities.
Improvisation, or the ability to think in paint, so natural to Matisse,
was by no means typical of Simon. Unable to let himself go, he
seems to have had a longing for symmetry which translated itself
into pairs of creatures, birds or animals, placed opposite each
other as hieratic mirror images in an exotic décor. These are also
painted in heavy impasto, and the colours are chosen with an eye
to emotional effect rather than truth to life. The result is
unashamedly decorative (something denied by Simon) and vol-
untarily limited, as though some enormously strong impulse had
got so far and then stuck in his throat. He seems however to have
thought of these as his most significant work, for which his pastels done from life in the Zoo were mere studies. For me however it is these that are more moving, redolent as they are of the
double vitality of artist and subject.

In them there is a precision, delicacy and brilliance which is,
on close inspection, compelling. Mostly small, they have an
immediacy which reflects the sheen of a coloured wing or the
flash of a green tail. The lizard on a bed of stones is like a jewel

on velvet, and the extraordinary Russell's viper, coiled on itself in momentary meditation, is delineated as with a feather, but with a masterly understanding of its quiescent vitality. Birds, butterflies and fish have nearly all something of this quality, the softness of the pastel itself vying with the rich density of colour and the extraordinarily sensitive outline or silhouette seen against the intense blue of the Mediterranean sky or the arid ochres and greys of rock and stone. The tiny Egyptian views of obelisks and pyramids are also imbued with luminosity, as though the limitless spaces of the desert and intensity of the sun provoked in Simon a state of total receptivity.

Just as he was *à cheval* between English and French culture, he felt torn between the impulse to surrender himself to the subject, and its opposite, the need to transform it into a formal design of his own making. It was his failure to discover a true synthesis between the two which renders his decorative pictures unsatisfactory. It is only in his portraits, well represented in the exhibition, that one finds not only an exquisite precision, but a deep need for essentials, a simplification and rhythmical understanding which underlines the nature and personality of his sitters. The instinct which, when he is designing rather than observing, betrays a certain rigidity, is here not allowed to take control, and serves rather to give his portraits an elegance and authority which are irresistible. It is indeed difficult to single out one from the rest, although the head of André Gide done in 1925 is particularly remarkable as a record of a singularly handsome and vivid, self-aware personality. By some indefinable magic Simon is able to suggest the deeper, less evident characteristics, often betrayed in the strange communion between artist and sitter. The large, fully realised portrait of his mother-in-law Lady Strachey, painted in oils, is also remarkable, as impressive as any tribute from one generation to another, on a par with Whistler's portrait of his mother.

In spite of one's assumption that Simon's life must have been enriched by his intimate connection with England, I find it hard to understand M. Pierre Rosenberg when he says in the catalogue that Simon's art is as English as it is French, even though in saying so I may be betraying a gross insensitivity. Although he painted landscapes at Rothiemurchus and portraits of the Strachey family, I cannot see any obviously English quality in Simon's artistic point of view. His intelligence, precision and intensity seem to me born from a rib of Degas, and have little to do with Turner or Constable – perhaps more with Girtin and Cotman, although the gulf that lies between pastel and watercolour renders such a comparison almost meaningless. Perhaps the connection can be seen in his genuine passion for landscape, of which there are some impressive and ravishing examples in the show.

The exhibition includes a number of photographs of students, Stracheys and others in which Simon's face stands out as an unconscious mirror of feeling, serious and engaged – in what, we, at this distance of time, cannot know – but he appears deeply absorbed perhaps by his own destiny, but at all events in something outside the claims of the moment, which is so interesting that he forgets himself entirely. It is the face of a man of tenderness and understanding, whose emotional life is one of great intensity. In the light of such an expression is is permissible to wonder about his intimate relationships, particularly with Dorothy and her family. What different worlds they sprang from and, superficially but not unimportantly, how differently his apprehension of the world in general must have been from that of the Stracheys. No doubt they had a good deal in common, particularly a rather stringent sense of humour. For the Stracheys the pole of reality lay in words and verbal discrimination rather than in the sensuality which was the mainspring of Simon's art. But here perhaps was a reason for mutual attraction. Even in France, once married, his life was led quite as much among writers as among painters.

And when he felt like it Simon could express himself in well chosen words, as when he describes his own painting, quoted in the excellent catalogue to the exhibition. It is perhaps regrettable that he did not write more. But in my memory his silences were almost as eloquent, brimming over with the unsaid, a kind of answer to the impressive articulacy of the Stracheys, hinting at passions beneath the surface quite as strong as theirs.

IX

House Painting

I left England for France in March 1984, at a moment when the structural repairs to Charleston were nearing completion. By the autumn of that year it was becoming clear that the exciting moment of restoring appearances, as opposed to the reconstruction of the fabric, was becoming imminent.

If I had thought or even hoped that I should, on account of living abroad, be left out of this enterprise, I couldn't have been more mistaken. The gentle voice of Deborah Gage broke in on my early breakfast one morning to ask whether I would consider a visit to England in order to repaint the rooms at Charleston and restore to them the colours with which I had been so familiar. I hesitated to say Yes, not because of the time and trouble involved, or because of the possible pain of seeing Charleston naked and divested of charm, but because I was still feeling overwrought from four weeks spent in Dallas, Orono and New York, unready for a further absence from France where my attention was mainly concentrated on doing up my own house, having almost reached the moment of painting its walls. Debo, however, was not only persuasive but needed any support I could give, while at the same time I was strongly tempted by the job, since I had strong feelings on the subject. These were mingled with what I supposed was a sense of responsibility, though I am aware that it is sometimes difficult to distinguish between this and a desire to prove that one knows better than anyone else. I did not allow such thoughts to preoccupy me, however, and set about putting my French house in some kind of order, buying a mountain of cat food and some other provisions for Mr and Mrs Stogdon who, on Debo's recommendation, were coming to house-sit. They would, I knew, have to put up with the compressor of the stone-masons and the hammering of the electricians, with the consequent dust from the stone walls which settled on everything in the house, as well as the incomprehensible jokes of the plasterer, who stepped straight out of a Provençale Midsummer Night's Dream. The weather was sulky and cold, hardly suggesting the carefree, sybaritic existence attributed to Provence and the Côte d'Azur; the percipience of a French friend, who had likened this neighbourhood to 'Les Hauts du Hurlevent', or Wuthering Heights, seemed more than justified.

I arrived in England on the evening of 29th March, a year and a week after having left it, and was soon plunged into committee meetings, the most pertinent of which to the present subject was one held round the kitchen table at Charleston with all the restorers except Danielle Bosworth: Philip Stevens for paper, Pauline Plummer for painted woodwork and decorated walls and furniture, Joe Dawes for architectural woodwork and Sarah Lee for oil paintings. Our immediate purpose was to define and agree if possible on the degree of finish to which we should try and bring the house. Exactly how glossy or how shabby should it be? For some time it had been evident that all those who had known the house well when it was still lived in, either by Duncan and Vanessa or Duncan alone, had different memories of its appearance. To each of us objects, furniture and pictures 'lived' in certain places and for that person that particular arrangement 'was' Charleston, an intense personal memory which, if someone else suggested it had been different, seemed threatened with destruction. Splendidly self-controlled though we were, one could hear notes of suppressed anguish rising to the surface from time to time, betraying the intensity of feeling within. It was evident that talking to one another produced an effect of stalemate, since no one was prepared to relinquish their private vision, while at the same time we could not put it into words or say why it was so important, still less why it was so much more important than anyone else's. A further difficulty was that, when anyone who had not known Charleston in its bloom asked for exact information, it was often impossible to be accurate, since Duncan and Vanessa were always changing things. Vanessa had a joke that whenever one of her aunts or cousins felt frustrated she started moving the furniture, and it may have been something of this sort that prompted her to follow suit – but it was also a creative impulse, since in their pictures painters are dealing with space, and moving three-dimensional 'volumes', as Roger Fry might have called them, was simply an extension of this mental activity. Each time the new effect carried with it the authority of perfect judgment, so that we who experienced the results could hardly remember the previous arrangements. I do not think I exaggerate when I say that each one amounted to a new discovery which provoked in the observer an emotional effect of a deep and lasting, if indefinable, nature.

It was with this kind of thing in mind that Debo asked Richard Shone to give us his idea of what Charleston should look like 'in the end'. I do not think she used that expression, but if she had one might well have asked: should there be an end? Should we not think of the whole process of restoration as a continuous experiment, treading as far as possible in the footsteps of Vanessa and Duncan themselves? Most of us would, I think, answer Yes to this hypothetical question, with the essential proviso that such an attitude should be subject to a high degree of sensitivity to the combined personalities of Vanessa and Duncan. Richard's answer to Debo made a very important point, bringing us back to

103

terra firma; he recalled that in the 60s and 70s, when he had first known the house, Grace was still the housekeeper. Fabrics and furniture might be threadbare and worm eaten, but they were clean and polished. The floor boards were her pride and she regularly visited every corner of the house, including the studio, with broom and duster. Though Duncan did no more decorating, every now and then a lavatory or a passage was given a new coat of colour by a local hand, and though elegance as understood by the professional decorator was never one of Charleston's attributes, freshness, cleanliness and order still emanated from every room. It was an order which had been instilled into Grace by Vanessa who, though artist and soi-disant bohemian, clung to the desire (more or less hopeless in view of the habits of her family) that she should be able to find things where she had left them, and the feeling that rooms had a public as well as a private aspect and should present, to the unexpected as well as to the expected visitor, an atmosphere of untroubled serenity.

It was evident that this view surprised both Phillip Stevens and Pauline Plummer. We realized that we had been over-emphatic in suggesting that in order to preserve the fragile and indefinable atmosphere of Charleston nothing must be restored to a condition of glossy newness, and this had left in the restorers' minds the impression that the house should look much the same as when they themselves had first seen it – in a state of advanced disrepair, even decay. It was a question of degree, and the mental cobwebs that hampered our vision began to clear as we realized that it would be inappropriate to buy manufactured ones and hang them from the corners of the rooms, or issue an invitation to the swallows to nest inside the front door. A middle road must be adhered to in which rigidity must at all costs be avoided, since each room and wall – indeed each corner – must be considered on its own as well as in relation to the rest of the house and, a still greater problem, in its relation to the past. Did we want stains of damp, worn and bumpy surfaces, dirty patches and smoke stains which had accrued with time – and, if accepted, had not been intended by Duncan and Vanessa – or did we want to put the house back to what could arguably be their own dream of perfection, where such things did not exist at all?

The answer to each of these questions was No. Common sense must be our guide, an attribute of which both Duncan and Vanessa had plenty; we must avoid insensitive perfectionism on the one hand and sentimentality on the other. Without making things look impossibly new, the aim should be to refer as often as possible to the aesthetic values that had been in Duncan's and Vanessa's minds when they had decorated the house, without denying the fact that time had played its part and contributed its own effect to what we thought of as the quintessential Charleston.

It was a relief to feel that we had arrived at a common point of view, but it was obvious that it would be no straightforward matter to put it into practice. The difficulties lay not so much in the changes of style between 1918 and 1936 or later as in keeping the homogeneity that holds them together; and the thought cannot but occur, who are we to imagine that we know the minds of two such spontaneous and instinctive artists? Both Quentin and I, the most intimately connected with the house and its occupants, have our own artistic personalities to hinder us; to hold a brush in hand amounts to an invitation to self-expression rather than the ability to lose one's self in the artistic personality of another, demanded by the art of the restorer. When the artists are your own parents, such subjective problems are increased.

On Tuesday morning however I felt full of self-confidence, happy at last to be in action. I thought I 'knew' exactly what the colours had been, a subliminal knowledge reinforced by the more objective memory that Duncan had told me that the so-called white on the walls of his bedroom contained both black and Burnt

Sienna. I also remembered that the walls of the spare room, with which I had helped Vanessa, had been painted with red lead mixed with white. I was familiar with the palette they had used and I was ready to go ahead as in the old days, pouring unmeasured colours into buckets, adding size as we used to say 'con amore', relying on an inner certainty to guide my eye and produce results that would have the same effect as the original.

I should explain that Debo had succeeded in getting the kind of colours that had been used in the first place, no longer commonly available. The basis was white chalk to give body to the colours, to which were added powdered pigments as required with an admixture of rabbit's-glue size to bind them together. The disadvantage of these colours from a practical point of view is that the binding agent is not 100% efficient; to some extent the colours always rub off, although traces of them remain for a surprisingly long time. In 1917 such colours could be bought locally and were extremely cheap. Nothing else, short of oil colours, would have been available, and these would have had a very different effect and cannot readily be used on either plaster or paper. To Duncan and Vanessa what mattered was the dry, chalky appearance reminding them of fresco. As the colour dries the white chalk seems to float to the top, leaving a powdery look like the bloom on the surface of a plum.

I started on the library, which I could remember when, as Vanessa's bedroom, it had no bookcases. Here the main part of the walls was black, partitioned off in each corner by bands of Venetian Red of varying width. Cornelissen had provided Mars Black and Ivory Black, with which I started to experiment. On either side of the window were narrow strips of the original colour and I set to work to mix and match the same. Mars Black proved too blue, so I mixed a black with Ivory; this was too warm. I spent the whole morning trying out various blacks on small pieces of white paper, accelerating the process of drying with a hair dryer, but I could not match the greenish tones of the original. At the end of the morning my self-confidence began to falter, so, knowing that misapplied effort only leads one still further astray, I turned to Clive's room.

Here I had an easy task to match the main part of the walls, which I knew had been painted with Yellow Ochre, although in order to get exactly the same colour I had to add a small quantity of Venetian Red. I suspected that since 1917 both Yellow Ochre and Ivory Black had changed, and that they vary according to the place they come from.

More subtle was the question of the Lemon Yellow beam which runs round parts of Clive's room. This struck a chord that had always surprised and thrilled me. I had never tried to reproduce it in another context, but it remained at the back of my mind as a possible experiment, and meanwhile whenever I entered the room struck me by its originality. Owing to my own oversight we had no Pale Cadmium and I tried to compensate for it with Medium Cadmium and Viridian. In a small quantity this looked very like the original, but when applied and allowed to dry merely reminded me of Lime Mousse. I eventually covered it with a transparent wash of cadmium mixed with size, which seemed as satisfactory a solution as could be managed.

The black for the library remained to be dealt with. In London the following day I compared a minute scrap of the original Lamp Black, but though the name was suggestive the thing itself was wrong. In the end I realized that the black was influenced by the minute green leaves of the wallpaper it had been painted over. I added Chrome Yellow, hoping for a greenish tinge: too little yellow made scarcely any difference, while too much produced a black that was not green but rusty. In the end I had to be content with mixing in a fraction of yellow which I put on in two coats and, as it then looked too solid, vigorously scrubbed off again with a yard broom. Having achieved this capacity to destroy my own work, a new mood began to creep over me; I had made a step in the direction of the true restorer.

At the same time I could not but ask myself not only what I was trying to do, but what ought I to be doing? In spite of my 'knowledge' of each colour, I had compromised in almost every case. I was reduced to saying it was a question of sensitivity – surely the last-ditch defence of the restorer, or artist, who does not know what he wants. But of course this is just what it is, though equally necessary is the strength of mind to stick to what you 'know' is right. This is the only way that the illusion, which we were trying to create, would be justifiable. As I worked, however, I realized that, in spite of the intensity of feeling that lies behind it, memory is fragile, unreliable and elusive, hating above all to be pinned down and brought out into the open, for a fear that it will be proved not a confirmation but a disillusion.

The experience illuminated the seemingly immense difference between colour-matching (something I now feel persuaded should be included in all artists' training) and the process demonstrated by Duncan and Vanessa whenever they dipped a brush into paint. I well remember Vanessa's slow, sensuous stroke and Duncan's delicacy of touch. Had they been matching someone else's colours – a thing they were perfectly capable of – their state of mind would have been quite different. As it was, to watch them painting a canvas or wall was rather like seeing a diver under water, or a blind man gazing at a vision obscured for everyone else. Colour sprang from palette to painted surface guided, it seemed, by instinct alone, and was seldom wrong. Until the following day, when they applied their minds to what they had done, the process was certainly not one of conscious thought.

In my effort to recapture these results instinct almost became the devil's advocate. I had to guard against it, never allowing it to take the bit between its teeth. Nevertheless I wanted to apply the colours to the walls in the same way as in the past, thickly so

that the brush marks would show and the colour underneath –
sometimes of a startling contrast – would glow through. As powder colours dry two or three shades lighter than when applied, it
often took a good deal of nerve to mix them strong enough. It
was some time before I could bring myself to shake enough Lead
Red (a new, non-poisonous colour which takes the place of red
lead, though in powder form it bears no relation to its seductive
forerunner) into the undercoat for Vanessa's garden bedroom. On
the wall it looked like cooked lobster, though it later paled to
salmon, a colour for which Nessa had a weakness but which personally I had never liked – a possible reason for my finding it so
difficult to deal with. A further problem was that, though we
used the same brushes, the marks left by myself were different
from other people's, and none was the same as Vanessa's and
Duncan's. Apart from the fact that our brushes may have been
different, we each had different nervous systems and moved to a
different rhythm.

When I looked into the studio to see how Pauline and her
students were progressing with much larger areas of wall than
any I had tackled, I was amazed to see that they were using sprays
and other sophisticated devices, and that their brushes were tiny.
I realized that nothing could be more different than our two atti-
tudes, mine crude and happy-go-lucky, Pauline's careful, knowledgeable, experimental and analytical. A combination of the two
was no doubt what we needed, provided that our two extremes
would meet.

There was one important difference in our situations, since in
the rooms I was doing at the time there were scarcely any extant
remnants with which to compare. Pauline, however, was painting one wall of the studio to match the remaining one, and, though
her task was full of difficulty, she had plenty of evidence to go on
until she came to the lime green over the door into the Folly,
which she had to 'imagine' – an example of successful concen-

tration. It may be said here that photographs, though useful from other points of view, were useless as far as colour was concerned.

I was amused to realize once more that the studio walls were painted only after the pictures had been hung, proved by their shapes exposed on the bare plaster. There had evidently been no question of doing anything so time-consuming as taking them down and hanging them up again. This was true also of the mirror which was bequeathed by Duncan to Clarissa Roche. When she took it away I was alone in the house, and painted over the bare oval in a colour not quite the same as the rest of the wall. Pauline and I discussed whether this should now be imitated. I could not help thinking that Vanessa and Duncan would have been rendered speechless with amazement.

It is indeed hard to guess their attitude to the process of restoring Charleston. Though hypothetical such speculation has an interest in reminding us that our proceedings are radically different from their own attitude both to life and to art, to the spirit in which Charleston was conceived and carried out, the very spirit which we are trying so hard to prevent from flying out of the window. Had they decided that Charleston needed 'refurbishing', a word they might have used, they would never have started imitating their own work, though neither would they have destroyed it. Incidentally, my daughter Nerissa tells me that long ago, when she was living in France, she painted a picture of the family sitting round the dining room table. Unable to remember the wallpaper, she wrote to Duncan to ask him to send her a diagram. He responded with a pattern that was deceptively like it though not the same: he had never bothered to go into the dining room to look at the original. Wherever possible they would have given things a new look, and who knows but they would have been delighted with emulsion, with paint that won't drip and even with sprays and rollers – though they would almost certainly have used them in an unorthodox way. This is the point at which we

are forced to part company with them and concentrate on repro-
ducing past glories rather than launching ourselves into experiment. In their serene evening mood, I think and hope that Duncan
and Vanessa – give or take some amusement both at our problems and at our way of dealing with them – would have been
secretly pleased that we care so much.

X

The Restoration of Charleston

When I first saw the film "The Restoration of Charleston Farmhouse" I was inevitably struck by the fact that the two people who are responsible for Charleston are conspicuous by their absence. This fact, obvious though it is, is brought home, paradoxically enough, by a film which celebrates their gifts. This it does with insight and discrimination, and perhaps it is only for me that the impact of such a film must forcibly recall presences that are no longer there. True, we are reminded of Christopher Mason's film about Duncan, and we see one or two snapshots of Vanessa. But we miss her presence, we do not hear her voice, and as I realize how narrowly she missed being filmed, and how easy a film would have been to make, in spite, probably, of her own protests, I regret the source of inspiration it would have provided.

Had we been able to see her, as we see Duncan, in the act of painting, her brush moving slowly, almost dreamily, across wall or canvas with sensual indulgence, we might have understood something of the spirit in which the decorations were conceived, as well as glimpsing the depth of her concentration. This was not so much intellectual as a state of absorption, almost of trance, all the more remarkable because at any moment she was liable to interruption from the cook, the children or the telephone. We might also see her, suddenly conscious of some omission, lift her hand to her forehead, leave on it a mark of red or blue, and exclaim at her stupidity. Whatever it was that had struck her as wrong – a colour left out or a dribble too much – she would certainly have found a way to adapt or improve the original, and continue what one might call her tightrope act, with serenity.

As things are, however, it is the house that, or – as I was about to say – who, has taken over. It is she who is now the personality, the centre of attention, and of whom, in this film, we have a portrait. She is mysteriously alive, with the life given her by Vanessa and Duncan, and proves to be still full of secrets, like some latter-day Sybil. But because she cannot answer our questions in words, we have to woo her with loving care and put ourselves into a state of sympathetic concentration, hoping to decipher her meaning. We can no longer talk to the artists; it is to the house that we must listen. If the message is wordless, it is nonetheless both potent and poetic and, because it is a question of images, of the mark on the wall, it is there for us to read with our eyes.

One of the reasons why we are seduced by Charleston is its evident fragility, which in itself makes it so different from a national monument, or at least from those other houses which are generally regarded as classic examples of their kind, confirming for us a whole epoch and maybe a whole class of people who, we suppose, lived 'like that'.

Charleston is not a museum piece: it is not a *pièce montée* which has been put into the freezer, waiting for our inspection. It does not tell us anything about a general way of life and cannot be taken as typically English. As decoration, it does not exhibit a fashionable style of the time: it is, rather, a one-off experiment, an example of individualism, pursued for its own sake, certainly not to impress the Joneses or anyone else, nor because it has a moralistic or political message, but because it was as natural for those concerned to express themselves in this particular way as it was to breathe. It is this breath of life the restorers are trying to charm into remaining with us for as long as possible, a task which, in some ways, is made all the more delicate not because we do not know enough about it, but because we know so much. The creators of Charleston inhabited it so recently that it is not so much a question of discovering or exposing their traces as of not obliterating those that remain.

In the case of an Elizabethan mansion or a Queen Anne house, the documentation of its inhabitants is usually sparse and impersonal. If we know what they did we do not know how or why they did it, nor which things they liked or hated doing. We have some idea of the style, but little of the idiosyncracies of their behaviour, and we usually only know how much they appreciated their houses in terms of financial value. The more they spent on them the more precious they were: but how much did they really like them? Probably a lot, but one cannot help feeling that they viewed these things with ineffable simplicity: they had not yet reached the age of self-consciousness.

In some ways not knowing these things makes it easier for the restorers, since life does not interpose itself between them and the bare bones of architecture or restoration. The restorer can peel off layers of dirt, burnish the gilding or sand down the wainscot, confident that he is giving back a lost glory, and that when he has finished we shall see before us a perfect work of art, something so perfect, so complete in itself, that we shall be awed into thinking 'Is it possible that ordinary human beings lived normal lives in such surroundings?'

But with Charleston it is not so. We may treasure the building because it is typical of Sussex; but neither is it unique, nor is it an architectural gem. If we want to save the house it is because of the life that went on inside it, expressed in such an extraordinarily individual way. Far from being designed by professional designers and architects who, after finishing their work, went off and designed something else, the house was decorated by those who lived in it and who, over the years, added to their decoration and even changed their style, again and again. It is very different from a house where every corner has been thought out in order to sustain a single idea. This is very satisfactory and beautiful, but it turns out that the opposite can be equally so: Charleston may be an amalgam of different styles, but the impression it leaves on us is benign, restful and holistic. We envy those who lived there for the gay, calm and luminous surroundings, even though these show no apparent homogeneity, and although there is not a straight line or right angle to be found anywhere.

This is another thing which makes the task of the restorer difficult. He or she can never relax, settle back on the ladder and reproduce a mathematically correct line on a cornice, or replace a worn out piece of wallpaper with a modern reproduction indistinguishable from the old. No doubt the skill required is as great in both cases, but Charleston requires more imagination, more sympathy with the aims of the artists. The restorers have been asked to make a great imaginative leap, a break with tradition, and to understand not only what the artists were trying to do, but what they refused to do. Even more unacceptably, they have been asked to devote their skills to restoring things that were never meant to be permanent.

Looking at Charleston today we are charmed by the gentleness, the softness of the colours and the freedom with which they are handled. These things are no longer shocking, because we have seen a plethora of art books, magazines and reproductions; our visual experience is too sophisticated and we respond to an effect that seems to us wholly natural. It may seem odd to remember, therefore, that Duncan and Vanessa were trying hard not to produce anything that could have been called 'pretty' or tasteful. They were intent on evading the laws of the interior decorator which tend to suppress a spontaneity that, for them, was infinitely more valuable. They did not set out with intent to shock. But if they happened to do so they were not above being pleased, since the ability to shock is proof of vitality. Life, when watered down by good taste, seemed to them not worth having.

But if, at Charleston, spontaneity was rated highly, it did not become an end in itself. Both Duncan and Vanessa had been educated in academic schools, and their response to the immediate sprang from the knowledge and discipline thus acquired. It was a bonus, an overspill from a general effort to liberate their lives, and therefore their surroundings, from all that seemed to them pretentious or dull, everything that still clung to a dead tradition. And at that time the most potent tradition was still that of William Morris, whose traces were everywhere evident and had become, by then, in many contexts, dreary and irrelevant. He himself said, 'My work is the embodiment of dreams, one way and another', but his dream had by then lost its urgency and become a sort of safety net protecting the innate conservatism of the English middle classes. Charleston is also the result of a dream, but, one feels, of a more private one than Morris's. Vanessa and Duncan were not didactic; if they had a vision, it was primarily for themselves, they had no intention of preaching to others. Not entirely devoid of social conscience as they were, favourable to the idea of the availability of art and against its being only for the rich, it did not follow that they wanted to impose their idea on the public at large: they were no crusaders.

Morris was a visionary, exalting his strong feelings for exquisite craftsmanship to a level where it became a symbol for a life of spiritual refinement and discrimination. His insistence on moral, political and literary elements was supremely English. He loved things for their own sake, intent on knowing what they were and why they were there, what their use was and why they

117

had been designed in that particular way. He appreciated them in their context, and when necessary re-created such a context for them, using his enormous practical and historical knowledge in order to do so. It is impossible not to respect such a vision, not to be touched by its innocence and simplicity, its faith in the past. But in some very important ways it embodied exactly what Duncan and Vanessa most distrusted, since what they were looking for was not the knowledge of what a thing is or how to recognize it, in other words a label. Indeed, they avoided such knowledge, searching for relationships, connections that exist beyond it, and that produce something unexpected. Where Morris was a perfectionist they were concerned with the aesthetic of immediacy, with a state of repeated or on-going experiment in opposition to Morris's cult of the past.

In another way also Vanessa's and Duncan's attitude to decoration was at the opposite pole to that of Morris. For them Charleston was not an end in itself, so much as an opportunity that had fortuitously presented itself. It was not so much a house to be decorated, and thus made into an entity that might continue to exist on its own into an indefinite future, as yet another canvas waiting to be painted. Their style as painters is repeated on walls and doors, on fireplaces and furniture, which explains why the brush marks remain visible, why accidents are accepted as felicitous, why colours are strong and uncompromising. It also accounts for the subjects chosen, the way they are seen, and for their references to the art of the past. For although they did not dream of identifying with the past, as Morris did, they were familiar with it: they saw the history of art with the eye of the professional who has looked long and keenly at the European tradition. They not only knew what they owed it, but viewed it with intimate love and affection. Much of what we see on the walls of Charleston emerges from this contemplation, often in the form or an ironic but appreciative commentary on some of the artists

118

they most admired.

One of the most interesting aspects of Charleston is this familiarity with a rich cultural tradition, combined with an awareness of the passage of time which belongs to the 20th century. Charleston is not only a fountain of vitality, springing from the earth of sleepy Sussex, but a protest against an excessively self-conscious desire for permanence and monumentality. In spite of its do-it-yourself air of holiday art – what Phillip Stevens calls 'fun art' – it is a perfectly serious statement that art need not be sententious, that we have reached an age when ephemerality is a more accurate expression of modern life than the longing for the appreciation of posterity. The beliefs of the Victorians were revealed as rather ridiculous, and the excitements of the present moment as spiritually, if not materially, more rewarding.

Nothing at Charleston was treasured for its material value and, until one of two of the paintings were discovered to be worth far more than had ever been imagined, which was not until the late fifties, thoughts of this nature appear entirely irrelevant. Duncan cherished anything that referred to Vanessa, while she treasured those things painted by him. Some things were more loved than others, and it is typical of their attitude that, when Clive sold his Vlaminck, Vanessa's reaction was to copy it before it left the house, and to hang the copy in place of the original, getting a certain pleasure from contemplating her skill as a copyist, even though it could never be the same. All the things they had picked up abroad in rag markets or junk shops were loved, in exactly the same way as everyone loves accumulated souvenirs: partly for themselves and partly for their associations. But they were also played with, rather as children play with toys they may have temporarily forgotten. Every now and then Duncan and Vanessa would be found, covered with dust and cobwebs, moving a pot or a statue so that it could be seen in a new and more favourable place, or in conjunction with some new gift or acquisition. Things took on new appearance, even a new life; placed in front of a mirror one would see them both from the front and the back, reflected against a newly painted wall, and one's old pleasure was enhanced by an appreciation of new possibilities.

Painters to the core, Duncan and Vanessa were primarily interested in appearances. These they found so compelling that they needed nothing else to stimulate their painting; they enjoyed the ambiguity, the constant changes, the unexpected relationships that become apparent if things are looked at for long enough with a sufficiently open mind. It was this that informed their attitude to Charleston as a whole: living there was rather like living on a stage where the set is being constantly changed or modified, and it is this that accounts for the nails that support the curtain rods, or the hundred and one expedients that were used to keep the tables from falling or the chairs from collapsing. As long as anything could perform a role in the general scheme of appearances, it was not discarded, although, in the course of time, it might go through a series of metamorphoses. Of course, this style of living is by no means exclusive to Charleston and its inhabitants; we all make do and mend, and it sometimes leads to the production of such exquisite things as patchwork quilts or rag rugs. But at Charleston practically the sole motivation was to satisfy the eye, and when this was achieved there might well be a move towards the paintbox, and yet another picture started in celebration of the visual effect. But it would be a mistake to suppose that this search for visual satisfaction led to a state of self-conscious exhibitionism. Both Duncan and Vanessa were well aware of the role that chance plays in these things; if they kept their eyes open all the time, if they changed and adjusted things, it was always in relation to what was already there, and it is for this reason that we will feel a sense of unity and wholeness about the house and garden.

One can say that Charleston was more Vanessa's creation than Duncan's, if only because a house is, or was, more likely to be a woman's province, and Vanessa had an exceptional ability to create an easy, happy atmosphere. It was not a question of '*le confort*', but a gift for visual harmony which, by suggesting that the mind was at peace, comforted the body. Given minimum warmth, a cushion or two, a curtain, a shaded light and a bookshelf, what more could you want – except of course an easel, a canvas or a wall to paint on? In the garden, for many years more or less neglected, the same feeling prevailed; here the primary requisites were a terrace to sit on and to suggest, perhaps, the *dolce far niente* of a southern climate, a lawn as a concession to people who like the greenness of grass, a pond for reflections and as many flowers as possible for their colour. Statues, gazebos, fruit trees and the like came afterwards. And indeed most of these things we owe to Duncan, who was more of a plantsman than Vanessa, longed for the unusual and the exotic, and whose dream, it turned out, was of a slightly different nature. As we know, he dreamed of flamingos, but at no time managed to install at Charleston more than two or three Chinese geese. And this hardly mattered, since he was quite capable of thinking he had seen an albatross fly past the window when it was in fact a sparrow. But it was he who bought and installed the life-size cast of Antinous (now disappeared) and the heads on the wall as well as the more unusual plants. Perhaps it was his childhood in Burma which induced this longing for something reminiscent of a sunnier, more Mediterranean, climate, a more Latin influence. It was, when one comes to think of it, of a totally different nature from Vanessa's vision, which was pragmatic, full of acceptance of things as they were, seeing poetry in domesticity, in daisies, snapdragons and red hot pokers. If she managed to keep Duncan from going beyond the bounds of possibility, she was also delighted by his fantasy, and finally, for our own pleasure, reconciled both extremes.

121

XI

Duncan Grant (1885-1978)

When I was 17 my mother Vanessa Bell, in the hushed accents of anxiety and love, told me that my father was not the man I had always believed him to be, but Duncan Grant. The deeper reverberations, like a bomb 1500 feet down, took many years to rise to the surface; at the time I had the sensation of some invisible but essential object clicking into place – a gap hitherto dimly felt had now been rightly and magically filled. To say however that it had been filled with a father figure would be untrue since, although I now knew who my father was, Duncan never for a moment behaved like one. He was more like some changeling uncle, or one of those relations in a Russian novel who mysteriously come and go, and whose existence though taken for granted is never explained.

As a child one looks anxiously at the grown-ups, hoping not to see the shadows that flit unconsciously across their faces, indicating their absorption in what is clearly an unnecessary sense of responsibility. On Duncan's face I never saw such an expression, he never wore the harassed look of those who hang their cares like an invisible chain of office round their shoulders, and this was in part the secret of his attraction, particularly for the young. He possessed the instinctive wisdom of an animal, never undertaking responsibilities that belonged to others, never promising more then he could perform. He bobbed to the surface, gently irrepressible, impervious as a duck to water, elusive as a leaf on a pond. If this appears to be egotism then Duncan was a consummate egotist, with a clarity of vision that is rare, doing neither more nor less than he wanted.

In the give and take of daily life however no-one could have been less self-centred; given the opportunity to paint during the hours of daylight and long after – I well remember the difficulty of persuading him to leave his easel even when his canvas was nearly invisible – he was absolutely open to the demands of children, friends and family, and disarmingly ready for any new experience. Such experience was seldom solitary; it was as though his daily communion with the apples and pears of still-life, having satisfied him, left him free for the ephemeralities of social intercourse to which he gave himself up, supported by a cigar and a glass of whisky, with the unselfconscious pleasure of a cat sitting before the fire.

And yet up to a point, which like one of his drawings had become exactly defined, he was resolutely loyal, absolutely dependable. He never failed to visit his mother and aunts once a fortnight, to see old friends who were ill or in need, to answer letters and to respond courteously to the young with a look of shining detachment, as though once he had fulfilled his real function he was free as air to gracefully perform any others. At the same time even Vanessa felt that she could or should not pin him down; at the back of her mind I'm sure there hovered the fear of escape. She herself might be caught in the meshes of domesticity, but Duncan would only hover beside her as long as it suited him, and only then as long as he knew he could flit away to other worlds when he needed to. Realising this Vanessa did her utmost to shelter him from interruption with the result that Duncan often perversely regretted the distraction she had tried to protect him from. He was eminently sociable, whereas she was not; he enjoyed new faces and personalities, whereas Vanessa found them disturbing, and could only respond with formal manners that had been instilled into her from childhood, which hid her like a cloak, saving her from unknown quicksands. If she kept her name out of the telephone book for Duncan's sake, it was also very much for her own. Leafing through the many little engagement books that until recently lay around at Charleston it is difficult not to sympathise; to judge from the amount of visitors who came to the house she was obviously fighting a losing battle, in the light of which the amount of work actually accomplished by her and Duncan is amazing. Her family the Stephens are said to have been congenital workaholics but so, without the concomitant sense of strain, was Duncan.

In my childhood I took Duncan for granted, but at about the age of 16 I began to understand that he was not to be so taken, he was too individual and unlike anybody else. With the hunger of the adolescent I fell in love with him and began to adore him; he was perfection and could do no wrong. His virtues, though apparently negative, were unusual and vital. He never asked for or demanded love, and when it was showered on him accepted it with naturalness and dignity; neither was he ever repressive or didactic. The lessons that he taught were given with a gentle take it or leave it air that allowed one all the freedom in the world to do either, and as a result even if I did not act on them I remember them. Once in talking about the theatre, I boasted of my ability to improvise in order to cover up loss of memory. By asking me whether I wouldn't find it better to put myself in a position to avoid such mistakes he pointed out a way of thinking which fixed itself in my mind as an alternative, especially when I became aware of the infinite pains and trouble he himself took about anything he did. True, he never tore out his hair or groaned in anguish, except in order to tease, but he was prepared to start

125

work over and over again if he thought it necessary. There were occasions when he admitted defeat: one I remember late in life when he was asked to paint the portrait of a deceased husband. After much trial and error he arrived at an impasse and, in some anguish gave me his picture and a photograph of the dead gentleman, asked me to do it for him! The results were deplorable, and as soon as she saw it the disappointed widow turned its face to the wall. I promised myself never to do such a thing again, but Duncan was simply happy to see an end to an impossible situation.

One of his favourite maxims was never to be ashamed, a lesson I remember learning in a droshki in Rome, returning to our studio after an evening's gossip in the Café Gréco. I forgot what produced my shame, and remember his recommendation mainly because it was so impossible to live up to; but I believe that he did so, having early realised that candour is the key to peace of mind. It is tempting to say that Duncan never disguised anything and that he was the most limpid and ingenuous of characters, but on second thoughts I am not so sure. Though apparently as innocent and guileless as a child, a wise and malicious smile sometimes flitted across his face, betraying an inner knowledge of other people's weaknesses and shortcomings that he otherwise kept to himself.

For me it was both welcome and extraordinary that he should appear so unruffled by Vanessa's powerful if unspoken reservations, the sense she gave of personal self-criticism which seldom allowed her to relax into unthinking enjoyment. Duncan was the only person who could persuade her to live momentarily in the present, sensuously enjoying her rare cigarette or cup of coffee, and making those ironical jokes that lit up the recesses of her mind. Devoted and entirely suited to each other as they were it would hardly have been possible, after the time they spent in each other's company, not to have sometimes affected each other adversely, like sealing wax that runs a little too far and leaves a mark when none was intended. Paradoxically enough Duncan largely avoided this by complete reliance on Vanessa, converting her into an oracle whose judgement was final and who was therefore placed outside and above ordinary human relationships. If he was thus able to protect himself by a combination of candour and innocence Vanessa suffered from the relentless appeal to her superior wisdom, willing as she appeared to be to shoulder the entire weight of both family and art. Feeling trapped and oddly lacking in confidence she responded with repeated appeals for reassurance, particularly with regard to her own painting, which she never ceased to denigrate in favour of Duncan's. Luckily he never suffered either from a swollen head or from a sense of inferiority; not being interested in analysing anyone's state of mind he was not of much help to Vanessa, and the relationship tended after a time to stick in the groove of reciprocated admiration.

After her death Duncan felt abandoned; no-one else could give him the same sense of security, or had that inimitable integrity which above all he appreciated. It was not as a lover or a wife that he missed her but rather as a combination of working companion and pythoness, a primitive statue engraved with a smile of bottomless tolerance and understanding. The figure in literature that came nearest his image of Vanessa was that of Dorothea in *Middlemarch*, maternal but exalted like the Virgin Mary, oddly unlike the voluptuous females that he idealised in his painting.

In his quiet and unemphatic way Duncan was full of courage. However unnerving it was to find himself unprotected and exposed he was not one to collapse or even I think to feel self-pity. He waited to see what would happen, and true to his instincts friends appeared, such as Lindy Guinness and Richard Shone, from a younger generation, heralding a host of others who, calling on his extraordinary elasticity of temperament, brought into his life a new gaiety, interest and appreciation. Appropriately enough it was the young who first re-evaluated his work, by then unpopular and forgotten. Once they realised that, far from being in his grave he was still alive and active, they responded to his unforced and natural sympathy, his spontaneity and gentle sense of humour with delighted surprise: was it possible for an old gentleman in his eighties to be so youthful and at the same time so full of wisdom?

XII

The Birthday Party

His hands, almost transparent, blue with the chill of extreme old age, lay on the coverlet, tips of fingers placed together, as in Buddhist prayer. They had lost their old capacity to dance a descriptive arabesque, cigarette held between index and middle fingers. Instead of gracefully describing, they acquiesced in passivity, like the hands on an alabaster tomb. In his face, the colour of mother-of-pearl, his nose still asserted its robust, eighteenth century shape. On the top of his fine, silver sprinkled hair was a woollen cap knitted in many colours, and his feet, protruding from under the blanket, were sheathed in striped woollen socks. On one of them perched a canary, which he was perhaps now looking at. His regard was oblique and one could not be sure.

Someone passed in the passage outside, looked in for an instant to see that all was well, and went downstairs to let in the sound of children's voices. "Can I, O can we – may we see him? Can we just say Hello? After all, it's our house! We want to welcome him." And another voice, steady, calming: "You must wait a little. He's asleep now . . . later on, later." And the tumult of voices, the rushing of small, energetic feet, so confident of goodwill, was all at once shut out by the banging of a door.

But the canary had been disturbed. It flew to the top of the rubber tree, the yellow of its wings reflected for a brief moment on the ceiling. The eyes of the old man did not follow it, but soon saw it again, perched on the other foot. He sighed, whether from contentment or otherwise, it was difficult to say.

There was a wheel chair in one corner of the room, a small table on which there was a block of water-colour paper and some brushes and tubes of paint; also a tumbler of water. A little canvas was propped up, showing a beginning: some red and blue splashes, some dribbles where the paint had run down. It was tentative, but one could see that it had a firm intention behind it. All round the walls there were pictures, and still more stacked in the corners. Plants and pictures – and books too in glass cases, well cared for, in good order.

The canary flew again, landing on one of the bookcases, dropping its liquid white excrement onto one of the tables below. Nothing else moved. There was no sound. It was as quiet as it is perhaps on the Moon. But it was not cold; the room was full of warmth and affection. It was waiting simply – for what was not yet clear.

On the bed he hardly moved; sometimes sleeping, sometimes blinking his pale blue eyes, that must at one time have been so large and so round. Now one could not be sure how much and how far they could see, and it was possible to imagine that, for him, the whole world was a conglomeration of blue, red and yellow dots, sometimes trickling or swimming together like marbled paper. Suddenly the eyes, a little glued up with the excretion of old age, opened wider: the canary had burst into song. It was twittering and chirruping and spilling out cascades of unpredictable notes in sudden ecstasy at something un-knowable. It was evident that the old fellow on the bed enjoyed it; he brought the tips of his fingers together in a little peak, and turned his head an inch or two towards the sound. But the bird was out of sight, behind a leaf of the abutilon that grew in the bay window. Perhaps it was the sudden gleam of pale sunlight that had set it off.

The day was drawing in. There was the sound of deliberate footsteps, the clinking of cups and saucers, a reassuring hint of tea time. The door opened and in came Swallow, his friend, bearing a tray with a teapot on it and the cups. "How are you feeling, Mischa? Want some tea?" and, putting the tray down on a chair, he took hold of the old man under his armpits, and sat him up against the pillows, as though he were Petrouchka. But Petrouchka smiled: "Whisky perhaps?" he said interrogatively. Swallow laughed. "Mischa, you old rogue," he said, "I'll put some in the tea. Then it will be Irish tea: you'll like that." Mischa laughed, very softly, wickedly, while Swallow poured in the whisky, and put the cup in Mischa's hand. But his fingers were not strong enough to hold it; tea and whisky spilled onto the sheet. "Oh dear!" he lamented, without really meaning it. "Never mind," he said, without quite meaning that either. Swallow wiped away the worst of it and held the cup to Misha's lips. He blew on the tea, intending to suck it in, and laughed again at his failure. "Mischa, suck," said Swallow, authoritatively. So he sucked, learning the trick quite fast. The whisky went down, what was left of it, like a treat. He leant back on his pillows and sighed again, quietly contented.

"And what will happen next?" he suddenly asked, as though out of the blue, just an idea that had occurred. "Mischa, you know quite well: it's your birthday party this evening. People are coming. Nettie has made some wonderful food." "Oh! I had forgotten . . . so I shall have to get dressed, and make conversation?" "Yes. But you have no need to worry. I shall dress you. And you know how to entertain people." Mischa lay back, evidently considering whether he could do this. For himself he was someone else: but he knew no one was likely to be able to understand such an idea. It was altogether too complicated.

Later on the children came in, squeezing shyly through the

131

doorway, excited because they hadn't seen him before, this very old gentleman who had come to live in their house. What difference would he make to their lives? Mischa was interested. He distinguished a thin girl, her fair, greenish pigtails hanging inert down her back: as he expected, the race of little girls had not changed in 80 years. There were white socks on all those fidgeting feet; above them knobby knees, unconscious of their similarity to those of ponies, trembling in a field. Mischa held out his hand, as though to show by the gentleness of his gesture the full extent of his friendliness. It seemed to surprise, perhaps intimidate them, and their readiness to smother him in their desire to share their delight in life was momentarily paralyzed. The girl touched his fingers with a formal politeness, and stood there, smiling a wan, embarrassed smile, while the two little boys stared, wondering and dumb. The canary, not to be left out, nearly had them laughing again by settling on the shoulder of one of them. But Swallow shooed them out, vaguely suggesting home-work or bed, and they went, relieved. Mischa was rather disappointed: was he too old for such encounters?

"But," he thought, "I was once like them, though I was a lonely little boy with neither brother nor sister. Only I had my Ayah, whom I loved, and needed no one else, really. She was so quiet, she had no self, only the desire to be everything to me; it would be nice if she were here now. When I was sent home at the age of seven, I wept – and so did she. I don't remember much but the whiteness of everything, especially the things she washed; and all the colours of the whites on the walls, and my mother's velvet dress, put on for parties." He seemed to float over those vast countries, India and Burma, bound in the far distance by the Himalayas, where there was a bear which had eaten his aunt. How his friends always laughed when he told that story, though there was nothing to it, nothing but this bizarre, surrealist fact, that she had been seized – and supposed eaten. Darkness descended. Someone came in to draw the blinds, and an unconscionable time passed, immeasurable, void. He was woken by Swallow, come to dress him for the party.

He sat in his wheel chair, his rainbow cap still on his head, a dark suit hiding his bones and a rug laid over his knees. His hands, now steadier, held a glass of whisky-on-the-rocks, and he was surrounded by a little group of people, talking more to each other than to him, joking and giggling. He regarded them with utter detachment, as though he were sitting at the summit of a mountain, and they were playing a game in the fields below. Sometimes he contributed a remark, eliciting much amusement, but though pleased, the laughter seemed to him to have little connection with what he had said. His eyes gazed at the blurred world in the far corner of the room. "Who is that over there?" he said, in wondering tones. "Oh, that woman," said a friend after turning briefly round, "Surely you recognise Isabel?" "Oh, Isabel," said Mischa, in tones of satisfied relief. "The last time I saw her she was sitting naked on a stone." The giggles surprised him. He went on: "By the swimming pool. I gave her a peppermint; I thought it might keep the flies away. But now of course she's different; she's changed a lot recently." And so there was a lively conversation, almost an argument. Everyone felt that Isabel had indeed changed; but how? And how uncanny that Mischa, so old and living apart, should have noticed.

Other people approached, and tactfully changed places. Old friends appeared as though by magic at his side, and one conversation slid into another, and even seemed to continue those begun many years before. There were no longer any gaps or tearings apart: only one continuous stream.

Food was brought. Plates on their knees, people caught Mischa's fork before it fell to the floor, wiped his mouth for him on the paper napkin, re-filled his glass and put it between his frail fingers. His face was suffused with a beatific smile, as he made less and less effort to follow the words, remaining outside and yet the cause of all that went on.

There were so many people now, the room was quite full. Groups were forming and voices became bolder, deeper, richer in tone. The women, some of them beautiful, were subdued and quiet, the men a trifle more booming; but all was very decorous. A group at the table were talking about Mischa. "But why after all shouldn't he do anything he likes? At his age – is it 93? – no harm can come. And he still loves life. Swallow took him to the National Gallery the other day: but if he were to die looking at a Cézanne, wouldn't it be perfect?" Now it was put so clearly, with such common-sense, all were agreed that Mischa had been free as air all his life and should not be hobbled or trammeled now. A delicate mechanism within him – something like the warning light that goes on when things get too hot – ensured his never getting stuck anywhere he did not want to be. One thing only counted, and that was painting; human beings were a game, an amusement, a play to be watched. If the actors thought, or made love, or quarrelled, it all took place on the other side of the footlights, while he looked on, often not understanding, but always fascinated. And sometimes he understood more than anyone realised, showing it by a shrewd remark or two which came as a shock to those who thought of him as merely a darling.

And so it was natural that the conversation was neither deep nor serious, and that there was a great deal of laughter on this, very likely his last, birthday party. Perhaps there is a proverb: gentle is as gentle does. It would have been suitable. And when Swallow wheeled him out to go to bed, it was almost as though a Yoghi was being carried shoulder-high through silent crowds saluting him for the last time.

When the morning came, he lay quietly awake, no need to be other than passive. Swallow arrived with coffee, later than usual, and found him extra lucid. "Ethel is coming today, isn't she?" he said. "Not Ethel, but Emily," said Swallow, used to the mixing of generations. "Oh yes, I mean Emily. When will she come?" "This afternoon, I think," said Swallow.

But when Emily arrived, who should have been but was not at the party, Mischa was speechless. Some slight infection had settled on his chest. He lay as before, hardly stouter than the stem of a plant under the quilt, the canary, unused to company, fluttering here and there. Emily sat rather rigidly in the rocking chair, unable, for the wrong reasons, to make small talk. His hand was too frail for her to hold, his appearance too remote for risking a hug. Feeling it was for the last time, she wanted to elicit a response, but could only get as far as realising that her stare was too much like a burden for him, so she sat, allowing Swallow to talk, oddly, of the future and of death. She was there perhaps an hour. It was no use staying – she had a long way to go, and it seemed wrong that she was returning to the house in which Mischa had lived, and which would never see him again, while she would rattle about in it like a dried pea. A column of granite seemed to be growing inside her, blocking every outlet, preventing both movement and speech. She looked at him, and saw that he was already more than half on the other side. What was left was no more than a pressed leaf. She rose and bent over him and, to her shocked surprise, heard a small, clear voice, saying: "Go home, my dear." So she went.

The room, when Swallow left it, became quieter and quieter. It suggested a bubble about to burst and dissolve into a little patch of iridescent moisture. The tension held for a little longer, for a little longer the breathing continued. But when, in the evening, Swallow returned, it had ceased. There was nothing left, nothing that is, that mattered.

135

Note

Child of a Bloomsbury now nearly mythical, daughter of painters Vanessa Bell and Duncan Grant, niece of writer Virginia Woolf, Angelica Garnett has remained true to her heritage and extended its influence. From her parents she gained her artistic strengths; and surely we may see a resemblance in her writing style, intensely observant of the life around her and at once precise and luminous, to that of her famous aunt. Music and theatre have also played their parts in her personal constellation.

Further, she has been a central force in the restoration of Charleston, the Sussex farmhouse in which she was born on Christmas day 1918 and which for many decades was the focal point of Bloomsbury in the country; in her memoir *Deceived with Kindness*, she has called it "the earthly paradise."

Besides her specific talents, Angelica Garnett has inherited not only from her family but indeed from all of what "Bloomsbury" meant and in idea still means, what we crudely call "the work ethic." How they worked! It was their Victorian heritage, which they were fighting against, that drove them to their desks and easels and settled them deep in rocking chairs to read and think before they changed at least England's literature, economy, art, and criticism.

Angelica Garnett has worked prodigiously, yet quietly, to ensure, to illuminate, and to realize Bloomsbury's legacy, even as she weaves her own legend into the brightly peopled tapestry.

She currently lives and works in Forcalquier, France.

—Constance Hunting
Orono, Maine

Puckerbrush Press
Selected List

Poetry

INTO THE AMAZEMENT   Deborah Pease
TO A VANISHED WORLD   Lee Sharkey
THE MOVIE QUEEN   Farnham Blair
LETTERS TO THE INTERIOR   Muska Nagel
CONSTELLATIONS OF THE
    INNER EYE   Sonya Hess
BETWEEN THE WORLDS   Constance Hunting

Fiction

AN OLD PUB NEAR THE ANGEL   James Kelman
A STRANGER HERE, MYSELF   Tema Nason
THE POLICE KNOW EVERYTHING   Sanford Phippen

Belles Lettres

NOTES FROM SICK ROOMS   Mrs. Leslie Stephen
ONE LITTLE ROOM AN EVERYWHERE:
    NOVELS OF BARBARA PYM   Lotus Snow
REMINISCENCES OF TOLSTOI,
    REMINISCENCES AND NOTE-   Leonard Woolf and
    BOOKS OF TCHEKHOV   S. S. Koteliansky
A CELEBRATION FOR MAY SARTON   ed. Constance Hunting
WRITINGS ON WRITING   May Sarton
THE EXPERIENCE OF ART:
    SELECTED ESSAYS AND INTERVIEWS   Constance Hunting

Corot.

What marvels - especially
until about 1845 - the Roman
ones Volterra, also Ville d'Avray
Rainy etc. -

Supreme master of
understanding terrain -
there's never a patch that's
vague or approximative.
Even when unskilful he's
always a painter, with a
feeling for values above all.
The more he feels the light
the less he uses colour,
the more restrained his
palette -

His colours seem to be
umber, Indian red or

in this intellectual sence
one is trying to do the impossible
that is interesting. Such is
the nature of man, & I take
it for granted, & it is of
course ~~due to~~ such
paradoxes that make the
~~occupation~~ endless fascination
of the work.

What is the relation of
the artist to his subject?
How far does he make
it, by selection, from
knowledge previously acquired
by influence — unconsciously
from temperament.